NELL NORAH JANE

Published 2021 in Great Britain by PostcardBooks
Part of EnvelopeBooks: envelopebooks.co.uk
A New Premises venture

PostcardBooks
12 Wellfield Avenue
London N10 2EA

© Jane Reid 2021

Jane Reid asserts her right to be identified as the Author of the Work in accordance with the Copyright, Designs and Patents Act 1988

Cover design: Stephen Games | Booklaunch

All rights reserved. No part of this book may be reproduced, stored or transmitted in any form or by any means, electronic or mechanical, including photocopying, recording or by any information storage-and-retrieval system, without the written permission of the publisher, nor be otherwise circulated in any form of binding or cover other than that in which it is published and without a similar condition being imposed on the subsequent purchaser.

A CIP catalogue record for this title is available from the British Library.

PostcardBook 2
ISBN 9781915023001

Designed and edited by Booklaunch for PostcardBooks
www.postcardbooks.org

Nell Norah Jane

A WARTIME CHILDHOOD

Jane Reid

Wartime *Punch* cartoons by Sillince
(William Augustus Sillince 1906–1974)

POSTCARD BOOKS

ABOUT THE AUTHOR

After graduating from Oxford, Jane Reid spent over thirty years as a diplomat's wife in eight countries. She was an Official Visitor to a leper colony in Guyana, lectured in the universities of Malawi and Cape Town and helped a wartime spy for MI6, George Tomaziu, to escape Ceauşescu's Romania with his family. On home postings she taught English in inner London comprehensive schools. After her husband's retirement she spent twenty years as an administrator of grant-making trusts. In 2014 she translated, edited and published Tomaziu's memoir *The Witness*. She lives in a quiet street in central London, near her family and her many friends.

Contents

Author's Note	i
1. Before the War	1
2. In Africa	10
3. Stolford	19
4. Boarding School	25
5. My First School Holidays	30
6. The War begins (*mostly in Somerset*)	35
7. My Mother, the Land Girl	42
8. Back to the Midlands	69
9. Growing Up	103
10. My Father	138
11. End of an Era	151

For all my wonderful children and grandchildren,
who ensure that in her old age
the long-ago only child is never lonely.

Author's Note

Nell the dog, my difficult Aunt Norah and the author on the lawn at Hollywood, the author's grandfather's house, in about June 1934

WHAT IS THE point of recording memories of my childhood? An archive for family and friends, of course, but also for my own pleasure: the pleasure of remembering early life as that alien being, one's self as a child—and an observant only child at that. Only children have more time for reflection.

In this book I have relived the things I saw, heard, felt, thought, dreamed, liked, feared and hated between the ages of two and twelve.

Between 1933 and 1945 I lived in many places and with many different people: in Birmingham with grandparents whose attitudes to life could not have contrasted more sharply; in rural Somerset; in colonial Africa; on an almost entirely unmechanised dairy farm near Bristol; and from the age of five at boarding school.

I was six when the Second World War started. All sorts of odd things began to happen and '... because there's a war on' became the explanation for everything—but of course we had no idea of what it was all about until later.

And then there was the whole daunting business of growing up.

By way of background, I have included some family history, showing how the Industrial Revolution enabled some of our more enterprising ancestors from different parts of the country to scramble into the middle classes—and record themselves in wonderful photographs.

It has been fascinating, illuminating and most satisfying to work on.

1. Before the War

MY FIRST MEMORY. Everything is white. A wall of white faces me. (It is the sheeted side of a high bed.) Far above me, a voice says, 'Jane! You mustn't jump on the ladies' tummies!'

I must have expressed dissent in some way, and the answer is crystal clear.

'Because it might hurt them.'

I feel cross. Jumping was fun and the ladies seemed to like it.

This strange memory is from 1935. I was not yet two, and a baby boarder at the nursing home where I was born, Oakengates, in Sutton Coldfield. I was parked there for five months or so in each of the first two years of my life while my mother went out to join my father in Africa. The ladies all had new babies—in those days, middle-class mothers spent at least a week resting in bed after childbirth (which can't have been good for them) and having a lively toddler to play with from time to time must have relieved the boredom a bit.

A few years later, when I was four or five, the sister of an aunt-by-marriage lost the use of her legs—for some unconnected reason—soon after having a baby. There was a lot of grown-up talk about 'poor Kathleen' and it somehow revived my very early memory. I felt obscurely that it must have had something to do with jumping on ladies' tummies, and perhaps it was my fault.

Resentment and guilt are powerful mnemonics.

IT WASN'T HEARTLESSNESS or neglect that landed me in Oakengates. My father, Lester Harwood, was a civil engineer working in Atbara, headquarters of Sudan Railways in what was then the Anglo-Egyptian Sudan. It was hot there at all times of year, intolerably so in the summer, with no air conditioning and little if any refrigeration. Medical services were limited, and very small children had been known to die. Only when I was two did my parents think it safe to take me with them to Africa.

Because of the climate all British officials in the Sudan were entitled to three months' home leave every summer, travelling to and from Port Sudan in Bibby Line boats, and their wives and families came home for longer than that. In 1933 my mother came back to England in good time for my June birth, but my father did not come at all. It was the worst year of the Great Depression and all civil servants (he was employed by the Colonial Office) had to take a cut in their pay, so he decided that he could not afford to take his leave; in truth he didn't like babies. My mother, who loved my father deeply, never quite forgave him for his absence.

When my father received the telegram announcing the birth of a daughter, his suffragi commiserated with him—'Oh dear! What a pity! Better luck next time, sir!' He met me for the first time in the spring of 1934, when I was nearly one.

MY MOTHER STAYED at home until I was about five months old and then it was time for her to return to my father in Atbara. She pushed me in my pram to Oakengates and left me there. She told me many years later that it was the hardest thing she had to do in all her life. (I should think it was even more painful in the following year when I was a toddler.) She also told me that she had tried to arrange for me to stay, with a nursemaid, at her family home—where she and I had been living since my birth; but her sister vetoed the idea 'because it might upset her social life'.

But why I was left at Oakengates and not with my aunt Gwen at my Harwood grandparents' house I never had the courage to ask.

THE HARWOODS AND the Alldays lived about a half a mile apart in the northern suburbs of Birmingham, and the families couldn't have been more different. I remember them all, and—minutely—every corner of both their houses.

Hollywood, my Harwood grandparents' house, was old and rambling, historic even. It had once been a coaching inn, The Bell, on the old main road from London to Chester. It had a huge and wonderful garden, and everyone living there loved me—especially Auntie Gwen, my father's sister, who was my guardian when my parents were away. I know I spent many—even perhaps most—afternoons there in those first two years of my life, and it is the setting for another early memory—perhaps even earlier, because there are no words.

I'm wearing a white smocked dress and coming down the stairs, very carefully, holding someone's hand—step by huge step. Grown-ups—Auntie Gwen, my grandmother, someone else—are eagerly waiting for me below. Now I'm standing on the bottom stair, their skirts are soaring up in front of me. But I know I'm going to spoil things, and I do—I'm sick all over my nice white dress and the red-tiled floor of the passage.

Later on (or perhaps it's another day) I'm sitting on an old gentleman's tweedy lap playing with his silver watch and chain. He is my Great-Uncle Frank Larkins, the rich uncle after whom my father had been given the first name Frank: fruitlessly.

A BIT LATER, in the spring of 1935, my mother has come home and the scene has changed to the Allday family's tall Edwardian house, 18 Greenhill Road, built by my other grandfather in 1910 next to the golf club in what was then almost country. I don't have the same warm feelings about it. The people who lived there—my grandmother, my mother's older sister Auntie Lorna and her husband, Uncle Nick—didn't take much notice of me. Even my mother was brisk and matter-of-fact in contrast to Auntie Gwen's gently concerned love.

I'M VERY SMALL and at Greenhill Road. I'm sitting on my potty on the square first-floor landing, shuffling it around on the brightly patterned carpet. Sunlight floods through the big stained-glass window on the stairs, throwing colour everywhere—red, gold, blue, green—and there are shimmering criss-cross sunlight circles on my wee in the pot.

When I am a bit bigger, I sit on the lavatory itself, clinging on to the seat with both hands. It's quite frightening. What if I fall in and the water whooshes me away?

IN SEPTEMBER THAT year, our 'South African' cousins came to stay (in fact, they were from Bulawayo). Mostly I remember lots of excited talk about it all, but I have a quick mental snapshot of the family standing in the garden. There was a boy a year or two older than me who must have made a big impression on me. Years later—I was seven or eight I think—he somehow became part of a dream which sustained me in an odd way through the vicissitudes of my childhood. I'm rolling down a hill—the fairway from the first tee at Walmley Golf Club to be precise—and I'm out of control, I can't stop. But then a tall boy of nine or ten appears, wearing a brown knitted jumper with a collar—lots of boys wore them then. As often in dreams, he bears no resemblance to photographs of the four-year-old visitor from Rhodesia, but I know who it is. He steps out and picks me up in his arms and saves me. For quite a long time, however lost I felt, I could take refuge in the dream, and I knew that in the end I'd be all right.

(Forty-five years later I visited Bulawayo and met the boy again, Kenneth Macdonald FRCS, a surgeon and leading citizen of the town. He was quite unlike the boy in my dream—he was stocky and looked just like my granny.)

IT IS THE spring of 1936. I'm nearly three, and my mother and I have just arrived back in England from my first winter in the Sudan. I'm curled up on the leather chair beside the gas fire in the back room at Greenhill Road, feeling ill. On the other side of the room the grown-ups are discussing what's wrong with me … . It must be chickenpox, my mother says, because one of the children on the boat had chickenpox. Once again, as with my first memory, the words come straight from the moment. But it wasn't chickenpox, it was measles, and for days I lay hot, uncomfortable, bored and lonely, in my mother's big double bed in a darkened room on the top floor. Shafts of light full of dancing particles slant through gaps in the curtains—they can't be opened wide because too much light when you have measles can damage your eyes for life.

MY EARLY MEMORIES of Hollywood and my Harwood grandparents are far more extensive. I feel important there.

I love Grandpa best. He puts on his panama hat and takes my hand in his, and we walk out into the garden together, past the hollyhocks at the side of the lawn, along the gravel path where a fuchsia dangles its flowers at my eye level—they're like tiny dancers, in billowing crimson and purple dresses—then round another corner and up the path to the greenhouse, where he picks a small sweet tomato for me to eat. Tomatoes were a newfangled plant when Grandpa was little, and people were suspicious of them because they belonged to the deadly nightshade family. The garden stretches on for ever.

Grandpa tells me stories about his own childhood in London. 'When I was a little girl …' he says. I'm almost certain that this can't be true and I squirm with delight in the complicity of a shared joke.

Nell, the dog, comes with us. She is a cocker spaniel, grey and black. She seems big to me—I am always surprised how small cocker spaniels are, because I was so little when I knew my first one.

Grandpa usually forgets my name: 'Nell ... Norah ... Jane!' he calls me.

A SHORT PATH leads away from the greenhouse—there are fir trees on both sides. It's rather dark and there is the faint sweet scent of pine. Auntie Gwen, irritatingly, calls it 'Jane's Lane', because that was what I called it when I was really small, before I can remember. (The grown-ups also insist on talking about a doll I named Corby, but I can't remember her either.)

At the other end of the path there is a summerhouse made of soot-blackened wood—it smells of coal dust and is not at all sunny. But it is home to a wonderful dolls' house which once belonged to my father's sisters. It's big, I have to reach up to the top floor, and it has a front door and five tall windows. When you open the front there are four square rooms each with the right furniture, and a hallway with a staircase that runs up, rather worryingly, not to a first-floor landing but to a blank ceiling. I move the furniture about and lose myself in making up names for the people who live in this magical house, and inventing stories about them. There are even tiny white vases that I can put flowers in—very little ones with thin stalks like the tiniest daisies. I can feel the vases now, their delicate curve and the textured smoothness of unglazed ceramic in my small fingers.

ALL OVER THE house there are things that belonged to those five long-ago children, my father and his brothers and sisters, who had lots of friends and lived a distant and charmed life in the early 1900s in a house called The Beeches. There is a set of battered cubes with jumbled parts of pictures on them—you

make a big picture by placing them correctly, and then, if you turn them over carefully row by row, another complete picture appears. And there is the flotilla of old lead warships that I sometimes play with after tea, lying on the drawing room floor and pushing them in and out of harbours formed by the arched legs of a little hexagonal Indian table with a pretty inlaid top. It's not much fun, but it's something to do while the grown-ups talk. The table sits in my living-room now.

A LEOPARD SKIN rug lies on the floor by the bow window. I know its story. My father shot it one day in the Sudan when he was travelling round the vast railway network to inspect the lines. This was in the 1920s; later, when big game hunting had gone out of fashion, he can't have been very proud of it.

Here, on the drawing room floor, it has a heavy head with glass eyes, and its red felt mouth is full of big white china teeth. It is very dead but I'm a bit afraid of it. Nearby on a low, round table sits a bright silver bowl with strange writing on it—Arabic, I'm told later. My father brought it home to his mother on his first leave when he was in his early twenties.

In one corner of the room there is a big shiny wooden chest which talks. Can someone be inside it? Is it Grandpa? At all events (a favourite phrase of his) Grandpa is magic. He conjures pennies from the air and from behind my ears and anywhere he chooses. Why does he bother to go to work?

Sometimes music comes from the shiny chest, which I soon learn is called a radiogram, and you put records on it—'The Teddy Bears' Picnic' or a man imitating the strange noises made by steam engines on the Great Western Railway line, as they double up and huff and puff up the Lickey Bank on their way from Bristol to Birmingham.

I have lots of books, including *Babar the Elephant* and *Babar the King*. I have a yellow dress made from material with pictures from Babar printed on it—the scene with all the little elephants playing in sand. And I have a lovely piece of soap with a picture of Babar going all the way through it. It lasts right to the end until the soap is hardly more than a disc with brittle edges to it.

AUNTIE GWEN, THE elder of my father's two unmarried sisters, and in her late thirties when I first remember her, is my second mother, the person who looks after me when my mother is away; but as often happens with someone who is there all the time, my picture of her is fluid and evanescent. I can see my grandmother clearly though. She is a stately figure and moves slowly. She wears dresses down to her ankles, usually nice soft blue material over something rather stiffer underneath. She has grey lisle stockings and low-heeled shoes with straps and buttons rather like my own. She doesn't say much, but she is a benign presence, and unquestionably the most important person in the house, more important than Grandpa, more important even than Auntie Gwen, who manages everything. Granny's place is always at the head of the table, and in the evening she sits by the fire with a glass of something with a faintly medicinal smell on the table beside her (it was a weak whisky and soda). When it's time to say goodnight, I lean up beside her and she gives me a butterfly kiss, flickering her eyelashes against my cheek, and there is a faint sweet smell of powder. You never get closer to her than that.

My aunt Norah, my father's other sister, is there occasionally. She is a Norland Nurse and usually away looking after other people's children who, she makes clear, are much more important than I am. Before lunch every day, someone takes me upstairs to wash my hands. I always hope it won't be Auntie Norah, because she bends my arms hard over the rim of the washbasin and then crunches the small bones of my hands together when she soaps them.

2. In Africa

From the age of two I spent the relatively cool winter months with my mother and father in what was then the Anglo-Egyptian Sudan, in the small township (now city) of Atbara that lies at the confluence of the Nile and the River Atbara, which flows down from the mountains of Ethiopia. Atbara is the headquarters of Sudan Railways and an important railway junction, where the line to Port Sudan on the Red Sea branches off from the main north-south line connecting Khartoum to Cairo.

Me with Mohammed and Osman

Years later, when I was in the sixth form at school, I became absorbed in Lowes Dickinson's book *The Road to Xanadu*, tracing the sources of Kublai Khan from Coleridge's notebooks and the books he was known to have read, obscure reference by obscure reference. Near the end comes the Abyssinian maid singing of Mount Abora—but where was Mount Abora? Perhaps, Lowes Dickinson suggests, the word could have come from a mountain in Abyssinia where the River Atbara rises before flowing down through the desert and into the Nile, at the point which the British were to make the headquarters of the Sudan's railway system. A poetic thought, but there was nothing very poetic about Atbara.

I am very little .... I am waving goodnight to Mohammed and Osman, the cook and the suffragi, as I climb up steps on the side of our domed bungalow to sleep on the roof—everyone (which in my world meant all the British) slept outside to escape the heat, on a roof or a balcony or even in the garden.

I am three and I'm stepping bravely and carefully on the first-floor rafters of the big house on the edge of the desert that is being built for us to live in next year. I look down between the rafters and see the floor below.

I am four. I'm in my small bedroom in the new two-storey house, and it's hot. I've had my lunch and my mother is singing me to sleep, 'Lazybones, sitting in the sun ...' she sings, and I watch, wide awake and astonished, as she drifts off even while singing.

Quite often I sit on her lap and study the funny grey mole on her left eyelid, or the V-shaped patch of sunburn on her chest where her frock doesn't cover her skin: it's red and looks a bit like meat.

I HAVE FEWER memories of my father. One afternoon he gets me dressed after my sleep and puts my frock on back-to-front—and already the implication is 'Well, men ...' (probably my mother said it). But it is also my father who shows me the stars and points Orion's Belt out to me. I still think of him when I see Orion in the winter skies.

He goes off to work very early, in the cool of the morning. When he has gone, my mother and I get dressed. We do our Exercises together, lying side-by-side on the floor. We raise our legs straight up in the air, first one at a time and then both together, and lower them very slowly, holding them up as long as we can—'to strengthen our tummy muscles,' my mother says. It's hard and rather boring. It's more fun at the end when we hoist ourselves up on our elbows and necks, and bicycle furiously in the air—I'm better at this than my mother is.

One morning, my mother and I are standing on the balcony after finishing our exercises when a woman rides up on a horse, and then sits out in the open, bareheaded, chatting to us. I'm shocked.

Even in winter the sun is dangerous. You have to put a solar topi on every time you go outside.

'She's not wearing a topi!' I cry—and my mother says that it's all right because it's only six o'clock.

We had horses and my mother's greatest pleasure was to take early

Me in a topi.

morning rides in the desert, but she had to give them up when I was around. I didn't have a nanny or a nursemaid so one of my parents—mostly my mother—was always with me, and desert rides were out. Oddly enough, I don't remember the horses at all.

After breakfast it's time to play outside in the shade, or on the veranda, or to go swimming in the pool at the Atbara Club. I have my lunch early, before my father comes home at about two.

'Here's the engine ... ,' my mother coaxes me as she tries to pop a mouthful in ... 'and here's the tender ... .' Usually I enjoyed my food, so it must have been something really nasty, probably slimy grey sheep's brains, which for some unfathomable reason were thought to be good for children. They were horrid and I refused to eat them. For many years afterwards I wouldn't eat anything remotely slimy.

EVERYBODY RESTED IN the afternoon. Life began again at about four o'clock, when it started to cool down. Social life for the Europeans in this small community in the middle of the Sahara Desert revolved around the Atbara Club, with the last two hours of daylight giving time for picnics in the desert or on the banks of the Nile, or a swim in the little pool; or, for the grown-ups, tennis, squash or golf (on a sandy course with greens of oiled sand) or riding. Every now and then there were races on the Atbara racecourse. The jockeys were small Sudanese boys; years later, to my utter astonishment, I found a jockey's outfit in a trunk at Greenhill Road.

After sundown there was bridge or snooker or poker—and dancing, flirting and whisky-and-soda—but of course I didn't know about this.

One afternoon my mother and I are at the Club, sitting at a table close to a high dark hedge, playing cards: Strip Jack Naked. It's the first time I have played cards and it's really exciting: I love the thrill of amassing a great pile of them—and then losing them, of near despair when you are down to your last few—and

then joy when a Jack comes along to rescue you … . The game ebbs and flows but in the end … I win! I have beaten my mother! (She was not the soppy kind of mother who always lets her children win.)

I TAUGHT MYSELF to swim in the small swimming pool, doggy-paddling across a corner, and then gradually managing a width, and then a length. Everyone thought this was a great achievement. One of my father's fellow engineers gave me a book to mark the occasion, a poem-story with lovely pictures. I had it for many years. The final picture showed a smiling woman with golden hair cascading over a long drapey apricot-coloured dress —ideal womanhood, pre-Raphaelite style, with angelic rather than sensuous overtones. I remember the poem that went with it:

> In your garden scatter seeds
> of loving thoughts and kindly deeds …

'Be good, sweet maid, and let who will be clever …' was very much the message to little girls in the 1930s. But, luckily for me, my parents didn't subscribe to it.

THINGS HAPPENED, AND an awaking consciousness of self. I have a sandpit and a swing in the shade at the back of the house. My only words of Arabic are something like '*moya fil gurda*', which is what I have to say to Hassan the gardener when I need more water to moisten the sand. One day there is a snake in the sandpit and I jump on the swing. It's frightening. Someone carries me away. My father, I am told later, shoots it.

From the upstairs veranda I watch Sudanese boys in their white galabiyas walking along a sandy path under palm trees on their way to school—and I think how lucky I am that I am English; and me.

In the cool of the evening we sometimes go for walks by the Nile. We watch men and oxen working a shaduf, a device for lifting water that is as old as time.

Mohammed and Osman are constantly in the background, tall and dignified in their galabiyas and turbans—but Mohammed is far from dignified one morning when we see him in the lane at the back of the house chasing a chicken, which doesn't fancy being lunch. The lane is sandy and bare—our new house was on the edge of the desert. The garden was pretty bare too, with

yellowy grass and a few pathetic plants pushing their way sporadically through the dry sandy earth.

We go to the zoo in Khartoum, where there are flat green lawns with wallabies hopping freely over them—and when I go back to Khartoum in 1954, it is just as I remembered it, so I think my snapshot memories of Atbara are accurate if not very illuminating. (Penelope Lively, my exact contemporary, whose Jacaranda Oleander tells of her prewar and wartime childhood in Cairo, remembers free-roaming cassowaries on the lawns at Khartoum Zoo: the same experience but different animals.)

A book arrives, *Kings and Things*. It's grown-up, it's history and the stories are true. I like it.

I stand up in the bath and pile my soap-suddy hair into peaks and study myself in a small square mirror.

At Christmas there are children's parties. One is my party—I have photographs of it, but all I remember is being kind and helpful to a little girl, Elizabeth, who is shy. I coax her to come out from behind some bushes and join the party—and have the satisfying feeling of being good.

There is a Sunday school party too—I remember being in a jostling group of bigger children getting ready for what must have been a nativity play. I haven't the faintest idea of what is going on, except that it seems to have something to do with camels.

THERE IS A lot of travelling. My three winters in the Sudan mean that I made six journeys on boats of the Bibby or Henderson Line to and from Port Sudan.

One day we go out in a glass-bottomed boat to see the coral in Port Sudan harbour. It is fantastic—a world of fairytale beauty, with the multicoloured coral like a garden under the sea and bright fishes swimming around it in the clear water. The vision stays with me all my life, but the beautiful coral does not survive.

Twenty years later my husband Martin and I, on our way to Burma on a Bibby Line ship, went out in the same glass-bottomed boat. The coral was still there, but cement from harbour works had killed it, turning it into a skeleton-garden, all white and grey. There were no fish any more and the water was milky.

On some of the ships you had to bath in horrid scratchy sea water with a small basin of fresh water to wash your face in—but I loved the swimming pool, and the special deck for children where we played on our own, away from the grown-ups. When we travelled to and from Burma with our own children, I was appalled at the small and uninviting netted-off area in which they were supposed to be confined—but when I was four I thought it was paradise, and even made it the start of one of the many books I started to write when I was nine or ten.

I remember one departure, probably in 1938. My mother and I are being driven in an open car across the desert near Port Sudan at sunset. I hold a small white shell against my knee: it looks just like a blister. I draw my mother's attention to it, but she is not impressed. When we arrive at the harbour, it is inky dark and the ship looms above us with all its lights sparkling. Later, having installed ourselves in our cabin, we stand on the deck and watch the lights of Port Sudan fade away. By the time we go to bed it is 11 o'clock.

ON ANOTHER VOYAGE, my father was with us and we made the journey shorter—and more interesting—by getting off the boat at Marseille (known firmly as 'Marsales' in those days) and then continuing by train. One evening, we visited some people called Mr and Mrs Love who lived in a flat high above the city. I had not been in such a tall building before and I remember toiling up endless stairs and seeing Mr Love's bicycle leaning against the wall by the front door of the flat ... and then we went out on to a balcony—and there, spread out beneath us, was the vast shimmering city and the sea and the port with its ships and the surrounding hills, under a huge starry sky.

In my next memory we are in the train, having breakfast in the dining car. My memory selects what mattered to me most. My father and I order boiled eggs, and when they arrive there are two each—but my mother takes one of mine away and gives it to him. He has three and I am left, indignant, with only one.

3. Stolford

THERE IS ANOTHER backdrop—a whitewashed cottage in the straggly fishing hamlet of Stolford, not far from Bridgwater in Somerset, which my parents bought to be our home for ever. We spent three pre-war summers there.

'Are we nearly there?' I remember asking for the umpteenth time as we near the end of our long journey from I don't know where. I'm sitting on my mother's lap on the front seat of an open car (as children did then) and getting more excited with every minute.

'Nearly,' my mother says—and this time it is true. We go through Stogursey and then twist through country lanes to the beginnings of Stolford. We turn right at the Chedzeys' shop, and then left by the house with the green shutters into the narrowest lane of all. I peer through the windscreen—'There it is! There it is!' I cry as we catch a glimpse of white through the hedgerows —and then it goes out of sight again until we draw to a stop right beside the white garden wall with the green door in it, and I scramble out and through the door and along the stone-paved path into the house that is our home for ever.

The cottage was called Sunnyside and lay sideways to the lane hidden behind a high white wall. From the front of the house you looked across the garden and a low stone wall into the field beyond. There were flowers and vegetables and cider-apple trees in the garden.

From the gate, the first door you passed opened into a stone-flagged barn, then came the dining-room window, and finally the green-painted front door. Inside, there was a narrow hall with doors to the dining room and the sitting room on either side, steep stairs with a hard coir carpet in front of you, and a short passage which led to the kitchen at the back. There was no gas or electricity or piped water—one of the grown-ups had to pump water every day from the well, which was in the barn together with the cider keg filled by a local farmer in return for our apples. The lavatory was downstairs—dark and frightening, and smelling of Jeyes Fluid. There must have been oil lamps for lighting, but I remember the house only in daylight as it was always summer when we were there. Six o'clock was my bedtime and however early I woke it would have been after sunrise.

BEING PUT TO bed so early, whether I was ready to go to sleep or not, meant that as an only child I spent a lot of time alone with my imagination. My bedroom was over the front door, with just about enough space for my bed. It had a cream cotton counterpane with greenish pictures of wild animals hand-blocked on it. This was worrying as real lions and tigers were probably lurking underneath ... so I had to be careful when putting a foot out over the edge of the bed. I remember a vivid and frightening dream in which my calm, stately Harwood grandmother—of all people—and I were clinging to the branch of a tree, with a fierce fox barking at us from below.

MY MOTHER DID the cooking on a coal range or an oil stove. I remember her saying 'damn' one day when the oil stove filled the whole kitchen with smelly black fumes, and the sponge cake she was trying to bake came out a floppy grey circle—rather like a dirty dish cloth. I'd said 'damn' once and I got into trouble—but in retrospect, if that is all she said, she was remarkably restrained.

All household work would have been similarly laborious; the washing done by hand, and ironing with a pair of flat-irons which had to be heated alternately on the range. A teenage girl from Stogursey, Sylvia Arlott, did some cleaning and helped to look after me. She and I used to ride in the dickey of our snub-nosed brown Morris two-seater—a dickey being essentially a bottom-hinged boot with some sort of seat in it. Once, I was even allowed to ride in it by myself—for a very short distance.

Stogursey was the setting for an ongoing bedtime story my father used to tell me, about a little boy who lived there called Gerald (his youngest brother's name). Gerald was a boy scout and had adventures. I nearly believed the stories were true.

One day—it must have been in 1937—I fell headfirst down the stairs and landed on the golden coach (but not the four horses) from the Coronation set that had just been given to me, and I'd left lying on the floor at the bottom. I was hurt, not seriously, but I was upset at the loss. To console me, someone bought me another set, so in the end I had the full eight horses that the real King had for his coronation.

THERE WAS A succession of visitors at the cottage: Auntie Gwen (*above*), grandparents, other uncles and aunts, and friends of my parents, but none of them had children and I had no one to play with except, occasionally, Bertie Chedzey from the village shop.

We went for picnics to lovely places on the Quantocks, but it often rained. My optimistic mother would scan the clouds looking for a patch of blue big enough to make a sailor's pair of trousers, and as soon as she spotted one—off we'd go. But her forecast didn't always work and sometimes the patch of blue never appeared at all. The only picnic I really remember was supposed to have been at Cottlestone, but we ate it at the dining-room table.

From the cottage we could walk to the sea, along the lane, across a thistly meadow (prickly for toes in open sandals) and over a high bank of pebbles on to a deserted beach, with patches of sand interspersed with pebbles, seaweed and mud, where we swam naked—even, to my horror, some of the grown-ups. The sea itself was the liquid mud of the Bristol Channel, enriched from the nearby estuaries of the Parret and the Brue.

There were some cottages by the thistly meadow, and Old Mrs Brewer lived in one of them. She had a broad, red face and whiskers, and sat by her front door with her legs sturdily apart and a huge sacking apron suspended between her knees, picking shrimps at a speed that astonished my mother. Sometimes we bought potted shrimps from her, delicious tiny sweet shrimps in salty home-made butter.

A MEMORY OF fury and resentment sets a moment in amber. I have been smacked for being naughty and then made to walk down to the beach, holding two grown-up hands. My chest heaves and wrenches with uncheckable sobs. My father tells me to stop crying because it's all over ... but it isn't all over, I can't stop, and my sense of injustice smoulders. (It was quite normal in those days for parents to smack—not beat—their children if they were naughty. But it often made the victims very angry.)

ON MY FIFTH birthday, Grandpa gave me a may tree and it was planted in the garden, which made the cottage even more my home for ever—but this was not to last: in the spring of the following year, when she was in England on her own, my mother sold Sunnyside: it must have been lonely for her when I was at boarding school and there were no visitors about.

Grandpa planted another may tree for me in his garden in Birmingham, but that had to be moved when the air raid shelter was built. Not a great success, my may trees—and not a brilliant choice for a little girl who would be at boarding school in May from the age of five to seventeen. Like the ship's play space, though, Sunnyside glowed in my memory and when I was nearly twelve and writing a composition for the Sherborne School for Girls scholarship exam, I wrote a half-fact-half-fancy story about the village shop in Stolford, and the Chedzey family who ran it. It is probably what won me the scholarship.

IN 2013 I went back to Stolford for the first time. Sunnyside itself had acquired some bulbous bay windows and wasn't pretty any more, but the straggly fishing hamlet had hardly changed. Standing by the sea wall, I got talking to a man of about my age. The men of his family had from time immemorial spent their working lives pushing wooden contraptions called mud-horses across the mudflats at low tide, catching shrimps, plaice, sea bream and other fish—they were plentiful in the old days, he said, but now ... . He was long retired, but his nephew was still pushing his mud-horse across the flats—the very last practitioner (according to *Farming Today* one morning in 2019) of a unique and ancient craft.

There is another change: the pebble bank we used to clamber over for a lonely swim is now topped with a concrete path leading to Hinkley Point Atomic Power Station half a mile away, and people come from Bridgwater to exercise their dogs.

4. Boarding School

FOR THE NEXT seven years of my life, from five to twelve, my most permanent abode was St Christopher's School, Rectory Road, Burnham-on-Sea, Somerset, England, Great Britain, Europe, World, Universe. Alternatively, Burnham-on-Mud or even, when we were feeling especially witty, on-Gas-Stove. It was an excellent preparatory school for girls (and pre-prep for boys) owned and run by the Misses Watson; Auntie Wattie and Miss Pat we called them, the first awesome and motherly, the second a bit shrill but a teacher without parallel. It laid the foundations of my good education.

But however good a boarding school is, it is not the right environment for a small child, especially for an only child who has spent nearly all her time with grown-ups and has not acquired the skills of getting along with other children.

When I'm with a five-year-old now, I sometimes try to visualise myself in those early days at St Christopher's: alone, a very small child abandoned by everyone she knew, bewildered, in a strange place with strange rules, strange children, and nothing familiar to comfort me. There were some swings in a dank-grassed corner of the garden by the kitchen door and I never liked them. I was probably sent out to play on them when my mother took me to the school in September 1938, and then someone must have come and told me that she had gone—no doubt she couldn't face saying goodbye to me. I can't remember the moment, but I can feel it, and I always hated that corner of the garden. (And there was a much better swing somewhere else.)

I CRIED A lot. In 1980 I went back to the school for its Golden Jubilee celebrations. A woman a little older than me said, 'Oh yes, now I remember you—you were the little girl who was always crying.' Even forty years on it felt like an accusation, and it hurt.

The unkind word 'cry-baby' still resonates, but then, in 1938, although I was all by myself and struggling in a life that was entirely strange to me, I was not conscious of blaming anyone or feeling particularly ill-used, nor, although unhappy, did I question my fate. Things just happen to five-year-olds: they have no options. Most of what I remember from that first year are moments of satisfaction—standing out, I suppose, from my general state of bewildered loneliness.

Magic Pillows was one of them. Three of us slept in a room for the real tinies called The Piggery because there was a frieze of the Three Little Pigs round the wall. We invented a game. We wee'd just a little bit on the sheet at the head of our beds and then put our pillows on top for a moment and, behold! the little yellow pool had vanished. We were proud and mystified. Nurse must have wondered why that end of our beds and our pillows were so stained and smelly.

And I liked being clever. The Kindergarten teacher was called Miss Butt, and she was renowned for being good with children. I was rather afraid of her though, and felt that she didn't like me—perhaps because I was a cry-baby, hinted at in my first school report: 'To begin with, Jane was apt to be very easily daunted by difficulties, and always wanted help to overcome them... .' But it went on to say that I soon improved. I learned to read quickly and by the spring I had become teacher's little helper, moving my chair round the class and helping other children through 'The Three Billygoats Gruff' or whatever dire story they were trying to read. And once a week in the summer term I was allowed to skip one of the reading lessons and spend the afternoon doing Painting with the Second Form instead.

THE SCHOOL CONSISTED of two large houses linked by a footpath, and the Second Form's classroom was in the smaller of them. To get there, I had to walk along the gravel path between them, only about twenty yards—but it meant that I had to go into the cloakroom and Change My Shoes, taking off my Indoor Shoes—with bars and buttons—and putting on horrible Outdoor Shoes with fiddly laces, so difficult for small fingers. Then I put my indoor shoes into a shoe-bag and carried them with me to the cloakroom in the other house, where I had to go through the whole difficult and tedious process all over again. Sometimes Nurse or one of the Big Ones—enormous girls of ten or eleven—was there and would help me, but often there was nobody about, and then I had to manage by myself.

(Once, when she was nearly ninety, I asked my mother what single thing had changed most since her childhood, wondering whether she would say cars, or radio, or television, or aeroplanes, or supermarkets ... . 'Mud', she said—the mud that was everywhere before roads were tarmacked and footpaths paved, the mud that made Indoor and Outdoor shoes a necessity.)

THE SUMMER OF 1939 was hot and for weeks on end we had meals and lessons outside under the trees. There was a boy called Michael. He was eight but not as clever as us six-year-olds. He would tip his chair over backwards and shout, 'Sorry Mrs Lorry!' and he and we would all fall about with laughter. We liked him and thought he was funny, but we knew he was different.

There was a tennis court between the two houses and beyond it a kitchen garden where you could hide under the nets and eat raspberries and unripe gooseberries; and a ramshackle wooden garage with a loft where apples were kept and where one afternoon a boy called Tom Holt rubbed some rotten ones in my hair, which had just been washed. I howled my way back to Nurse and had to undergo the shampoo-in-the-eyes ordeal of having it washed all over again. He was the first of the very few people in my life whom I have hated.

On Sundays we walked to St Andrew's church for Matins. In summer we took a path across the meadows, wearing pretty dresses and hats. In the summer of 1939, my Sunday dress was a sort of crushed strawberry-and-cream colour, and my matching straw hat had flowers on it. We held buttercups under each other's chins. If there was a yellow reflection it meant that you liked butter. I did.

MOST AFTERNOONS, SUMMER or winter, we walked down to the beach in an untidy crocodile, nibbling bitter leaves from the hedges along the way. We built sandcastles and canal systems and bridges and played games like 'The Captain Says'. Later, when we were bigger, we played team games on the good hard brown sand, pulling our hockey sticks along the sand to make the lines, and piling up bundles of seaweed as goalposts.

The tide went out for miles, the beach sloping gently away and the sand changing imperceptibly into liquid mud and then into the muddy liquid of the Bristol Channel, thickened, as at Stolford, by mud brought down by the local rivers. Even so, in summer, we went swimming whenever the tide and weather were right. To begin with I was the only Little One who could actually, if inelegantly, swim. The water was brown and the waves broke into cream foam, but it didn't do us any harm—no doubt because we were careful to do as we were told, keeping away from the patch a couple of hundred yards along the beach where the seagulls used to swim, because, the grown-ups said, that was where the town sewer came out.

From 1938 until after the war, the brown sea of the Bristol

Channel and the grey sea of Cardigan Bay were the only seas I saw and I assumed that the blue sea was just another grown-up story like Father Christmas: I lived on the sea, and it was brown.

5. My First School Holidays

I SPENT MY first Christmas holidays, in 1938—and many others later on—at Hollywood. I slept in a blue-carpeted room at the top of the stairs. It was really Auntie Norah's room—there were lots of photographs of the important children she looked after as a Norland Nurse—but I felt it belonged to me (this caused me problems later). There were blue silky curtains and a slippery matching bedspread, and a picture of a bluebell wood over the bed. Beyond the window, and the wide expanse of the once-main road from London to Chester, was Sir Josiah Mason's Orphanage, a huge Victorian building with a clock tower. It gave me a nice cosy feeling when I lay in bed and thought about all those dear little orphans just over the road—but, as in the Sudan, I knew I was lucky to be me.

Breakfast was the best meal. I sat beside Grandpa, our backs to the warm glow of the gas fire. We each had a boiled egg and toast—'a little bit of toast under my butter,' Grandpa said, lavishly spreading butter on a mouthful of toast (to spread a whole piece at once was somehow 'common').

After breakfast he would sit down by the fire and change his slippers for highly-polished shoes, using a long tortoiseshell shoe-horn to ease his heel in; the grown-ups remembered that when I was really little I had called it a 'shorn'—how silly, I thought. On special days, Grandpa would put spats over his shoes (was that what the long-handled button-hook that also hung by the fireplace was for? I can remember the object, but not him using it.) By the time he stood up he was the picture of elegance with his white moustache, gently curled and waxed at the ends, and his silky white hair with pink scalp glowing through it. He washed his hair every morning with Pear's Soap.

Grandpa had a stock of 'heartless rhymes' which were supposed to be funny—forerunners, I suppose, of Hilaire Belloc's *Cautionary Tales*—and they must have had the nursery rocking with laughter in the 1870s But I didn't like them. They had a sort of Grand Guignol approach that never appealed to me.

> They came to Mr Jones and said
> 'Your servant's cut in half! He's dead!'
> 'Indeed,' said Mr Jones, 'Then, please,
> Bring me the half that's got my keys!

Callous but practical. Others were downright puzzling:

> Young Billy, in his best of sashes,
> Fell in the fire and was burnt to ashes.
> Now, even though the room grows chilly,
> We haven't the heart to poke poor Billy.

Billy, in sashes? I found this far more troubling than the poor boy's improbable fate.

> Eating more than he was able,
> Tom died at the breakfast table.
> 'If you please,' said little Meg,
> 'May I have his other egg?'

His other egg? Were children allowed two eggs at breakfast in those far-off times? I felt envy towards Meg far more than pity for Tom—and how had he managed to overeat so early in the day?

CHRISTMAS DAY STARTED early. 'You can open your stocking when you hear the Orphanage clock chime seven,' Auntie Gwen had said (it did not chime during the night). When I woke up, it was still dark but I could feel an unfamiliar weight at the end of the bed. I reached out and groped for the stretched and cornery shape of a filled stocking. I listened intently. What time was it? The wind soughed through the trees, but faintly through it I was certain I could hear the chimes, ding-dong, ding-dong, and then ... one ... two ... three ... four ... five ... six ... seven. I jumped up, put the light on and attacked my stocking. I must have made a noise because within a minute or two Auntie Gwen appeared at the door, looking strange as she always did without her false teeth and glasses. It was still the middle of the night, she informed me, and I had only imagined the chimes. Reluctantly, I got back into bed and went to sleep again.

My main present, at breakfast time, was a new teddy bear. I liked him, but I didn't want to be disloyal to my old one, a battered and semi-hairless pink teddy whom I loved. In the end I called the new one Teddy and decided the old one was a girl and called her Susan, and loved them both. I can't remember when or where in the end I abandoned them.

The climax of our Christmas Day was tea-time. We sat at the table in the dark formal dining room—my uncles and aunts and my little cousins; even my Allday relations appeared at some stage. There were sandwiches and scones and cakes and jellies —it was a feast.

Afterwards, we all, servants included, gathered round the Christmas Tree which stood in the square hall in front of the family portraits. I had helped Auntie Gwen decorate it with fragile Christmas balls and bells and lanterns and strips of tinsel, which had to hang straight down so that they looked like icicles. Now, the lanterns were lit and there were lots of presents in brightly coloured paper hidden between the branches. With mounting excitement, I helped to distribute them. But they were little presents, and always rather disappointing. The only ones I can clearly remember were the special dolls given to the maid and cook, which were made of dishmops with a duster and a dishcloth tied round their waists to make skirts. I coveted the dolls at the time, but when, a generation later, I challenged my aunt about these dour presents she was quite surprised, and said she was sure the maids had something else as well. I hope so.

The maids I remember from those pre-war days were called Winnie—she did the cooking—and Vera. There was a nice gardener called Wall whose base was the potting shed in the garage block. It had a peculiar sweetish smell that I didn't like much—now I recognise it in John Innes compost, but I'm sure he made it himself. He was a young man and he joined the RAF at the outbreak of war and a grumpy old man called Hill took his place. Wall came back for a while when he was demobbed at the end of the war, but he soon got another and better job. (The men who worked for Grandpa were always known just by their surnames. Was I told to say Mr Wall, Mr Hill? I don't know—and I probably didn't say anything.)

Also in the garage block was the wash-house, which only came to life on washdays, when it was a dangerous place, hot, and filled with steam and the peculiar smell of boiling cotton. Another woman, called Martha I think, came in to help Vera with the washing. Using blocks of Sunlight Soap, they would rub the sheets and pillowcases up and down on corrugated wooden washboards, and then heave everything into a copper boiler that was prodded and stirred with long wooden poles. Then each item was rinsed several times, folded, and fed through the huge wooden rollers of the cast-iron mangle in the corner. You had to keep your fingers well away as they turned the wheel—otherwise, they warned, you might come out flattened like the washing on the other side. Later, at school, there was a girl whose arm had got caught and badly damaged in an electric mangle when she was little, which proved that the danger was real.

After all this, the two women hung the washing out on the clothes-lines criss-crossing the yard, and then pushed everything sky-high with clothes-props so that the washing billowed out or sagged from the lines depending on whether there was any wind or not. Sometimes in winter everything froze stiff, the sheets crackled cold in your fingers, and Grandpa's long combinations and shirts looked just like bodies hanging heavy on the line.

I have no idea what happened to all the washing after that.

6. The War Begins

Mostly in Somerset

PEOPLE A LITTLE older than I am remember with clarity the moment war was declared on 3 September 1939. But I was six and it was all mysterious to me. 'The war' was simply a word that was supposed to explain all sorts of sudden changes in my life.

I do remember the day, though—I wasn't very well and had been put to bed even earlier than usual—and then my father appeared in my blue bedroom with a present for me: a bicycle. This was because he was leaving—the war meant that he had to go back to the Sudan sooner than was expected. I was puzzled, but pleased about the bike.

The next day, like children all over the country, I was evacuated. Alongside my small cousins Robert and Sally, I was whipped off to Worcestershire to stay at their other grandmother's 'country cottage', an enormous black-and-white farmhouse in the village of Abbots Morton. Their grandmother had nine children and numberless grandchildren, all of whom had taken refuge there from the expected German blitzkrieg. The house pullulated with people, all, except for my cousins, total strangers and much older than I was.

In the daytime it was bewildering but exciting: people were kind, and there were horses and dogs and lots of things to do. The high point was when a Stop-Me-and-Buy-One appeared in the lane, a man on a big tricycle with a cold box full of ice cream over the front wheel. 'Buy one now! Now or never!' he cried: he was going off to be a soldier the next day. We bought ice cream sandwiches—little slabs of vanilla ice cream between wafers. And it *was* now or never. I didn't see a Stop-Me-and-Buy-One ever again, and it wasn't long before ice cream itself disappeared from our lives.

At night, though, for the small outsider put to bed at six o'clock on a mattress next to the banisters on the top landing, the house was full of terror. There were hours of shouting and laughing and talking, and coming-and-going and banging of doors, and even when at last it grew dark and everyone settled down to sleep, each moan and creak of the overloaded ancient house reached me, and kept me in fearful wakefulness.

Even so, it was fun in the daytime and I was quite disappointed when my mother appeared after a day or two to take me to another country refuge. We drove off in her new BSA Scout, a dashing sports car which she had bought the day before, for a bargain price 'because there's a war on'. Her staid Harwood in-laws regarded this as all too typical of her lack of seriousness ... she had gone to the shops to buy a pound of butter and come back with a sports car ... .

Our destination was the village of Spaxton in Somerset, not very far from Stolford, where my parents had friends with a son, called Ken, a bit older than me. We stayed there until it was time for me to go back to school.

I learned to ride my bicycle at Spaxton, first of all precariously for short distances on the lawn, then more adventurously on the lane outside. Finally, my mother took me for a cycle ride. On the way back there was a long hill and she warned me over and over again of the danger of going too fast —'You must keep your hands on the brakes until I say let go!' she called out to me. It was exhilarating. The air rushed past me, the gravelly road whizzed below, and my hands gripped the brakes as I waited for her command.

'Now!' she called—and I let go, only to find myself flying

head-over-heels on to the gritty road, ending up in a sorry heap of cuts and grazes on the ground. She was apologetic—she had not reckoned on the much faster speed at which smaller bicycle wheels go round.

After she had picked me up, comforted me, and dabbed at damp points (tears from my eyes, blood from my knees) there was nothing for it but to climb back on to my now slightly wobbly bike and cycle painfully back to base. It all confirmed my feeling that my mother was an exciting companion, but not safe like Auntie Gwen.

I WENT BACK to school soon afterwards. Nothing seemed to have changed at first, but 'because there's a war on' quickly became the standard explanation for why this or that thing or activity had suddenly become impossible. I remember pulling on a sheet of toilet paper and a token falling from the roll. Collect so many, it said, and then you could send them away and get an encyclopaedia. But I knew that because there was a war on it wouldn't happen.

To begin with, it was rather fun. We sang songs, parodies of popular songs of the day, suitably bowdlerised, and all of the utmost innocence and optimism:

> Run Adolph, run Adolph, run! run! run!
> Don't let the tommy have his fun! fun! fun!
> Bang! Bang! Bang! Bang! goes the tommy's gun,
> So run Adolph, run Adolph, run, run run!

and

> They're hanging out the washing
> on the Siegfried Line—
> Have you any dirty washing, mother dear ...?

and

> Underneath the spreading chestnut tree,
> Mr Chamb'lain said to me,
> If you want to get your gas-mask free,
> Join the blinking ARP!

We were all given Identity Cards, which we had to keep with us at all times—my number was WOBB 125/8 (my National Health number for many years thereafter).

We were also drilled with the routine of the air raid sirens—as soon as you heard the anguished up-and-down wail of the alert, you ran for the air raid shelter, and only came out at the sustained high note of the all-clear. The wailing of a siren still strikes a chill in anyone who was in a real air raid, even though nowadays the all-clear signal is what you hear.

Then there were gasmasks: an air attack with gas was the biggest fear. We were lined up in the gym and shown how to put them on. You pulled on the rubbery mask so that it covered your mouth and nose and stuck round the edge of your face. It had a transparent window so that you could see where you were going. Then you dragged the wide rubber bands over the back of your head, pulling your hair but making the whole thing airtight; now you were breathing through the filter in the nozzle. Once you'd got the thing on, you had to wait, breathing laboriously, with your face getting sweaty and a horrid smell of hot rubber, until one of the grown-ups came and tested it by holding a piece of paper to the nozzle. If the paper stuck there when you breathed in, it was working properly. We had to carry our gasmasks everywhere, but they were so much part of our everyday life that soon we didn't really think about them—and luckily we never had to use them. Some exceptionally spoilt day-girls had Micky Mouse gas masks, and the rest of us quietly despised them.

ANOTHER THING WE had to learn about was the black-out. Such cars as there were crept about on dimmed side-lights and you

'Now you must be careful with the blackout, Iris. If even a tiny chink of light shows there's the danger that the air-raid warden will see it … .'

must never allow even a chink of light to be seen after dark. Most windows had extra curtains made of cheap black cotton with an acrid smell of black dye and Air Raid Wardens snooped about checking that all windows were properly blacked out—any glimmer of light would be enough to guide a German bomber straight to the house.

Air Raid Wardens wore navy-blue uniforms and tin hats. Men in the Home Guard wore khaki uniforms and looked like soldiers but were usually a lot older—just like Dad's Army, in fact.

We were also drilled with the routine of air raid sirens. As soon as you heard the anguished up-and-down wail of the Alert you ran to the air raid shelter and only came out when you heard the sustained high note of the All Clear.

Quite soon, people began building air raid shelters in their gardens or even putting bomb-proof cages (Morrison Shelters) in their houses, and very soon they built an air raid shelter at St

Christopher's—Burnham was a long way from London, but not far from Bristol and even nearer to the Cardiff docks just across the Bristol Channel.

The shelter was built as a corridor linking the school's two houses—a great advantage, saving us from the vexatious ritual of changing our shoes. There were bunks on each side of this corridor, and we slept in them for months on end during the blitz—and indeed later, whenever there was any perceived danger of attack. Another advantage (for the Big Ones) was that the shelter ran along one end of the tennis court and provided a good flat wall to hit balls against. For us Little Ones who were put to bed soon after six, this meant enduring the irregular thuds of ball against brick as the Big Ones played into the light evenings of Double Summer Time. When we were bigger, we made good use of it in our turn.

WE WERE FERVENTLY patriotic without having much idea of what it was all about. We sang militaristic hymns with great fervour, and even as a little girl I felt deeply (and I still feel) the solemnity of 'For those in peril on the sea' with its magnificent sombre tune and metaphorical resonances.

It was especially important to me because my Uncle Jack was in the Navy, and my mother had been a Wren in the First World War. 'Worse things happen at sea,' she would say darkly whenever I complained of any mishap (which put things in proportion) and she made sure that I observed all the proper rituals: if you spilt salt you must chuck a few grains over your shoulder to avoid bad luck; and a sailor would die if you allowed a glass to ring without stopping it with your finger.

There were other children whose fathers were away like mine, most of them in the army, but one was a prisoner of war taken at Dunkirk, and later another disappeared from Singapore and no one knew whether he was dead or alive. (He turned up, emaciated, at the end of the war; in the meantime, as the rules dictated then, his pay was stopped and the family would have been penniless if the Watson sisters had not found a job for their mother at the school.)

A MAM'SELLE APPEARED. She had a pale, round, slightly puffy face, and dark wavy hair. She was weepy and we must have been unkind to her for we received a serious talking-to. She had had to leave her home in France ... she had lost her family ... she was very sad ... . The memory is a dim one and I can't remember the detail of what we were told, but we felt ashamed and sorry for our unkindness. I don't think she stayed very long.

7. My Mother, the Land Girl

IN THE FIRST World War my mother, aged 17, had 'put up her age' and joined the Women's Royal Navy Auxiliary Service as a driver (she chose the Wrens because she liked the look of her legs in black stockings).

'Driving a Ford van now,' she wrote in a letter to her brother, 'but soon it will be Admirals in ROLLS ROYCES.' The cars of 1917 are today's museum pieces—and fiendish to drive. For one thing, there were no self-starters, so engines had to be cranked into life every time they stopped. A 'small boy' went with her to do this—jumping back into the seat beside her as soon as the engine started with a juddering roar. The 'small boy' was probably in his early teens—the school leaving age was twelve until after the First World War, and many of that generation's poor children were stunted from undernourishment.

She had a good time. For some months she was one of only two Wrens stationed at Greenwich Naval College. When she was discharged in 1919, she returned to Sutton Coldfield. But life at home as an unmarried daughter playing golf and bridge soon palled. She went off to London to do a secretarial course and worked there until she got married at the age of twenty-seven. She lived in Earl's Court, and always loved London.

Now, at the beginning of another war and with her husband far away, Phyllis Harwood, active, country-loving and happy to work outdoors, joined the Land Army and in the spring of 1940, after initial training in how to milk a cow, she was sent to do the dairy work at Green Farm in the village of Claverham, about ten miles from Bristol and twenty from Burnham. She didn't take any pay—I think this was a matter of maintaining her genteel status as well as patriotism—and to begin with she used her own clothes. But she soon swapped them for the sturdy corduroy breeches of the Land Army uniform.

I SPENT MOST of my holidays at Green Farm over the next two years. The war felt quite close to us there.

It was a 90-acre dairy farm, with a pedigree herd of Guernseys. The pretty white-washed farmhouse stood by the road with a lawn at the front and a big kitchen garden at the back. Behind it was the farmyard with its barns and cowsheds and other buildings, and beyond them the fields.

Five people worked on the farm: George Shapland, the gentleman farmer who owned it; Weeks, the cowman—who was young and rather handsome, with blonde curly hair and a racing bike; Mrs Weeks, his slightly dour and older wife; Martel, a Guernseyman marooned by the war; and my mother. Then there was Kitty Shapland, the farmer's wife and boss of the house, the children—David, a year older than me and Rosemary, who was two—and Priscilla Weeks who was about my age and had her hair in ringlets—and may very well, looking back, have been the reason for a rather odd marriage.

It was made very clear to us that Majestic and Challenger, the two handsome bulls, were highly dangerous animals, and David and I kept well away from them, but the cream-and-rust-coloured cows were gentle and had names like Daisy and

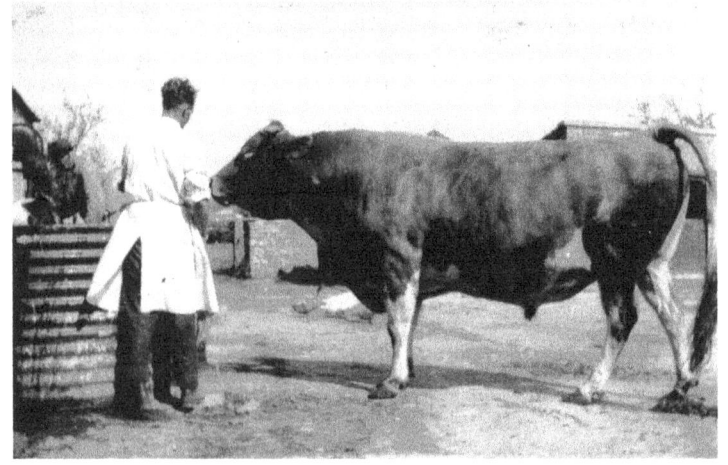

Buttercup. We sometimes ran alongside them as they made their slow and shambling way from the fields to the cowsheds for their twice-daily milking. There were chickens, ducks and geese, a couple of horses and innumerable cats who lived under the Black Shed near the gate into the vegetable garden.

Everything was done by human effort. The milking was by hand. There was a tractor, but the horses did most of the work, pulling the primitive-looking farm implements over the land; bigger machinery was hired when it was needed. Ducks swam on the duck pond. The hens scrabbled all over the orchard. We children used to climb inside the henhouses to collect eggs from the warm nests, but quite often the hens laid somewhere else, trying their best to keep their eggs hidden, and we had to hunt round the hedgerows to find them. The geese roamed freely too. They turned on young Rosemary one day when she was chasing them and took a bite out of her knickers.

My mother got up at 6.30, took Kitty and George a cup of tea in bed, and then went into the dairy to bottle the milk from the first milking. Weeks, Mrs Weeks and Martel did the milking, squatting on little three-legged stools, heads pressed against the cows' flanks, and then carried the pails of warm milk into the dairy where my mother lifted them high above the cooler and poured the milk into a funnel at the top; the cooler was like a freezing radiator of horizontally corrugated metal. The milk trickled slowly down over the ribs of the cooler and by the time it reached the trough at the bottom it was cold. Then she filled each bottle in turn from a tap in the trough before fixing aluminium tops on with a little hand-held tool—I was sometimes allowed to help with this.

When this was done she put the bottles into crates, which she lifted into a battered yellow van marked 'The Claverham Herd of Pedigree Guernseys TT'. The 'TT' meant 'tuberculin tested'—the milk was not pasteurised, and the cows were checked regularly by the vet to ensure that they were not infected with tuberculosis. She knew roughly how many bottles of milk she would need each day, and any surplus went into churns she would deliver to a depot in Bristol. When she had finished the bottling, she went in for breakfast.

Once or twice in the spring of 1940, during the so-called phoney war when hostilities hadn't really started, my mother made scalded cream. First, she separated the cream from the milk and then poured it into big flat pans set over boiling water. This was left for a long time to cool, and then the rich and unbelievably delicious sweet-smelling cream was lifted off—to be eaten on scones with jam. But such treats soon became a glorious memory.

After breakfast she set out on the milk round, and every now and then I went with her and helped her with the bottles. We went first through the scattered village of Claverham and on to the local small town, Yatton, where there were some big houses and a boys' prep school in a ramshackle, turreted house up a long steep drive. They always had bins of food waste, which we collected and took over to a pig farm. Then we drove into Cleeve and along the main road to Bristol, stopping at houses here and there in Brockley, Backwell, Flax Bourton, Long Ashton … . Not many families took Guernsey milk, which was extra creamy and cost more.

Last, we took churns of surplus milk to the depot, which was down by the docks. The road into Bristol sloped down a long hill overlooking the whole city—the docks, their quays and cranes, and a vast patchwork of grey buildings and shiny patches of water, dominated by three huge handsome red brick tobacco warehouses with 'W.D. and H.O. Wills' emblazoned on them. In the distance we could see the Suspension Bridge over the Avon Gorge, the Clifton Downs, and the terraces of Clifton itself. In the spring and summer holidays of 1940 it all looked very peaceful. A few barrage balloons were the only sign of change—like great soft silvery kidneys, they floated over the city to discourage enemy planes from dive-bombing this highly strategic area.

THE MILK ROUND—daily except Sundays—took up the morning, and after lunch it was time to start again. First, she unloaded the dirty bottles from the van and washed them, two-by-two, on fiercely revolving brushes in scalding, sulphurous water, before putting them to sterilise in a kind of oven. A bit later the afternoon milk would begin to come in—George Shapland often joining the milkers now—and she began the same process of cooling, bottling and capping—although this time the crates were put into the big walk-in fridge instead of the van.

It occurs to me now that Green Farm's whole income, supporting in reasonable style the Shapland family, the Weeks family and Martel, came from the milk my mother cooled, bottled, transported, and sold. It was lucky that there were subsidies.

Most of the time on the milk round, we were just being milkmen, leaving the fresh milk on the doorstep and taking away the empty bottles—but sometimes we were invited in. The first Aga I saw was in a house in Yatton, in a big warm kitchen with a splendid uniformed cook. My mother (*see facing page*) made friends with some of her customers—she played bridge with some of them and in other houses I was invited to tea.

Our last stop on the way home was Cleeve House, a dilapidated Georgian mansion at the end of the lane that led to the farm. It was full of evacuees from the East End of London, one family to a room. I remember the small children who came pouring into the hallway on our arrival, often half dressed, pale and grubby, staring at us as if we were visitors from another planet. The sight shocked my middle-class sense of what was proper, but I understood that these mothers and children were frightened and miserable. They were used to streets and street lights, and the narrow country lanes terrified them—if one of the women was brave enough to venture outside and saw the van coming down the lane towards her, she would leap into the hedge and pull her pram back as if we would otherwise run her and her baby down. These families came from a place that was, to me, unimaginably foreign.

I FITTED QUITE happily into the cheerful but rather haphazard life of Green Farm. Kitty—'Auntie Kit' to me (children then nearly always adopted grown-ups they were familiar with as aunties or uncles)—was only in her mid-twenties, good-looking, warm and strong. She had dark hair and a loud, laughing, cajoling voice with a hint of Somerset in it. Uncle George (not the most energetic of men) was less predictable.

David and I mostly mucked about on the farm, and I played with Priscilla sometimes—Rosemary was too little to be of any use. Sometimes, though, my mother would leave me to play at one of the houses on her round.

My favourite was the Eleys', a big house in Cleeve. There were two boys, Robin and Oliver, and we had great fun. We built a wonderful lair behind some outbuildings, using bits of old wood and corrugated iron. We even made a lavatory with a flush, fashioned ingeniously from a jerrycan, a length of hose, and some string. We didn't dare demonstrate it to the grown-ups. When I proudly told my mother about it as we drove away in the van, she said, 'What a pity! I needed to go.' Horror! How right I had been not to tell her! Like most mothers, she had an infinite capacity to embarrass me.

Quite often a rather odd young man loped round the walled gardens, never making eye or any other contact. He was the boys' uncle and, I now guess, autistic. But the term had not been invented then. We just said 'dilly'.

One Christmas I went to a rather grand fancy-dress party at the Eleys'. Someone had produced a pretty Hungarian outfit for me and near the end of the party we all had to parade around in a ring for our costumes to be judged. I wasn't at all sure what was going on, but I suddenly found myself in the middle, a joint winner, with everyone clapping—but then they drew lots for the prize and I didn't get it. I couldn't help feeling cheated. There was a marvellous conjuror who did wonderful tricks like producing somebody's watch from the middle of a ball of wool —this was the first time I saw him, but he kept on appearing at parties and even at St Christopher's during my years in Somerset, and his magic always enthralled me.

On another occasion David and I went to a party in Claverham Village Hall which was very frightening—long benches with rows of shouting village children and scalding tea from urns, which I had never seen before. After a bit I just left and ran home to find my mother, who was washing the milk bottles.

I RAN AWAY from school once, too. I was sent out of a French lesson and for some reason it was the last straw. I climbed out of the downstairs lavatory window into the coal-dusty yard at the back, crept along the fence behind shrubs, climbed over into the next-door garden and went out into the road through their gate. I knew how to get to Claverham. I had to walk to the end of Rectory Road, turn right into Stoddens Lane and then keep on walking until I reached the main road for Weston-Super-Mare, where I would find the road for Bristol ... .

By the end of Rectory Road, though, I began to feel tired and realised that the distance in front of me—about twenty miles— was going to be too much. Defeated, I turned back. At school they had only just missed me. I was scooped up into Auntie Wattie's comforting lap and given a sweet.

I wrote a poem at about this time (*see following page*). I can't have been more than seven. The handwriting is childish, but the spelling is good, and the apostrophe and indentations. My mother kept it. How could she have sent me back to boarding school?

> I WAS ALL ALONE
> I was all alone today
> I was lost.
> I could not find my way
> Back Home
>
> There was nothing there to do
> when I was lost
> O that I was with you
> Back Home
>
> But now there's lots to do
> not lost.
> O now I am with you
> Near Home

MY UNDERSTANDING OF the events of the war dawned slowly. 'Any relation of the famous admiral?' a visiting grown-up had boomed far above my head, soon after the Battle of the River Plate, where an Admiral Harwood commanded the fleet that sank the Graf Spree. At six I was baffled. I have no memories of Churchill's speeches or Dunkirk or the Battle of Britain—which happened a long way off. But everything changed when we drove into Bristol in the Christmas holidays of 1940.

The blitz had started. From the top of the long hill overlooking the town we saw grey smoke drifting from fires still burning after a raid the night before. When we got to the bottom it was a world in devastation. We went past warehouses and half-cleared bombsites, crossed the Avon by a swing-bridge and twisted right and left through a maze of bomb-damaged streets. Terraces of houses had huge gaps in them like wounds, their broken walls reminding one that people had been living there, perhaps till yesterday: bright wallpapers marking the different rooms, staircases going nowhere, fireplaces hanging in space, curtains fluttering in empty window frames, pictures dangling crookedly, and doors swinging lopsided and useless thirty feet above the ground ... and smoke everywhere, with its inescapable acrid stink.

Eventually we came to the milk depot, left our milk-filled churns and picked up empty ones before retracing our steps through the ruins. On another occasion, after a very big firebomb raid (I wasn't there), my mother got completely lost in the blitzed and smoke-filled streets, and, unable to reach the depot, ended up giving the milk away to exhausted firemen.

Altogether, 919 tons of high explosive bombs, and many thousands of incendiary bombs, fell on Bristol between November 1940 and the following May. There were 77 air raids, six of them major. Some 85,000 buildings were destroyed. Three thousand people died; many more were injured.

One day, as we drove into Bristol on the milk round, I saw 'START THE SECOND FRONT NOW' painted in huge white letters on the side of Clifton Gorge, and asked my mother what it meant. She didn't know. (It was in fact part of a Communist campaign to divert some of the troops from the Desert War to support the Russian army in their stand against the invading Germans.)

THE BOMBING OF Bristol brought things home to me—and Burnham-on-Sea was only just across the water from the mines,

'Oughtn't we to throw it back?'

steel works, ports and harbours of South Wales. Among the seaweed on the beach there was often debris washed up from wrecks—mines, bloated and smelly animal carcasses, bits of wood, clothing ... . Once some girls claimed they'd seen a drowned sailor, but I didn't see him and with my usual scepticism I didn't believe the others had either. On some afternoons, a plane would fly to and fro across the bay towing a target behind it for the local anti-aircraft units to practise their gunnery on. (Not much fun for the pilot, we thought). And there was another fear: invasion. The wide sand-and-mud beaches at Burnham sprouted ten-foot poles at regular intervals in every direction, to prevent enemy aircraft landing.

EVEN IN BURNHAM we sometimes heard bombing. I lost a pair of pyjamas when the Germans (probably off-loading bombs intended for South Wales) scored a direct hit on a laundry in Weston-Super-Mare. But Green Farm was only ten miles from Bristol and a few fields from the farmhouse there was a decoy—great piles of rusting oil drums which were ignited in the hope of diverting the German bombers from their real targets, the Bristol or Cardiff docks.

I REMEMBER WALKING with my mother down the lane from the main road to the farm one noisy night, I think in December 1940. Guns roared and bombs thundered, and the sky was red from a huge blaze somewhere on the other side of Cleeve Hill. I felt brave and excited, not at all frightened. According to my mother I instructed her to dive into a ditch if a bomb fell near us, and I would throw myself on top of her—I have no memory of saying anything so heroic. They must have told us at school that we should throw ourselves flat on the ground if we heard an explosion.

At the farm, when the raids were at their height, we slept downstairs, and sometimes the house shook with nearby bombs and gunfire. The longest and most destructive of all the Bristol raids was on 3 January 1941 and I remember—that night perhaps —lying on our mattresses in the darkened sitting room, and someone telling David to hold my hand to stop me being afraid. But I soon decided it was silly and pulled my hand away.

IN THE DAYTIME we roamed the farmyard and fields looking for bits of shrapnel. I had a good piece, a solid chunk of white metal —aluminium—smooth and rounded on one side, with a row of semi-circular bumps along one edge, and the other so jagged that I cut myself. We trekked over fields to see a German fighter that had been shot down and was lying rather pathetically near a hedge. The boys said they had seen the dead pilot before he was taken away, but, always sceptical, I didn't believe them—boys always said things like that, or shouted 'Messerschmidt', 'Spitfire' or 'Heinkel' at any plane in the sky. I didn't believe that they could tell the difference any more than I could—but in that case I may well have been wrong.

There were soldiers everywhere and you never knew what

you'd find when you went out for a country walk—'WD PROPERTY KEEP OUT' and sudden rolls of barbed wire blocking off the patch of woodland where you'd been playing last week; or searchlights; or a gun emplacement half hidden under bushes in the corner of a field: these would be anti-aircraft guns, and ack-ack they went as they fired away at enemy planes picked out by the roving searchlights that scanned the night sky.

These were all things we saw with our own eyes, but we had only occasional and well regulated news about what was going on in the wider war. There was no television to bring battles into our living rooms, and news in the papers and on the wireless (as we called it) was sifted through the Ministry of Propaganda (Was there really such a body? Perhaps it was Information) which gave a positive gloss to things whenever possible. Morale had to be kept up. Britain had to believe it could win. We children never doubted it. Mr Churchill was a hero with his V-sign and cigar. The King and Queen and the little princesses were heroic for staying in London and sharing the blitz; and the King did his bit by instructing his valet to put only four inches of water in his bath (but what was a valet? and why wasn't he in the army?)

Ignorance didn't stop us being patriotic. We sang jingoistic hymns and the popular refrains with great fervour, and my mother never let me forget my naval connections, making sure that I knew the naval rituals—and the importance of proper knots (a reef knot, never a granny).

Gradually, I began to understand a little more. But in spite of all the evidence—the soldiers, the guns, the bombs, the poles on the beach at Burnham—we children did not take the threat of invasion as in any way real, and the succession of defeats and disasters in 1940 and 1941 took place a long way away.

THEN THERE WAS 'The War Effort', a term used to explain all sorts of things and we children had to play our part. Early on, as part of The War Effort, people had to give the government their

'I suppose that after the war, they'll melt them down into saucepans again.'

aluminium saucepans (which were the latest and best in those days) so that they could be used to make aeroplanes, and the iron railings in front of houses and around parks were torn down to make bombs.

IN THE AUTUMN, the War Effort meant picking wearisome quantities of blackberries and rose-hips in the tall hedges that divided the flat fields around Burnham. The fields were intersected by dykes, wide drainage ditches that you crossed on flat wooden bridges. We were on the Somerset Levels but I never heard the term then. We knew, though, that somewhere nearby was the Isle of Avalon where King Alfred hid in the marshes and burnt the cakes, and we all felt part of a heroic tradition.

A penny from our pocket-money—which totalled around sixpence a week—now had to go on stamps for War Savings, and we joined energetically in various money-raising campaigns: Wings for Victory! Tanks for Attack! We made banners and held them up across the flat roof of the air-raid shelter and got very excited about the amount of money that we had raised. But I can't remember how we did it. Some of our efforts were also purely imaginary: we were intensely suspicious of a Spy, in the form of an innocent clerk carrying a briefcase who crossed the road in front of the school on his way to work every morning.

Some of us knitted but I found knitting boring and was bad at it. Anything I knitted was full of dropped stitches or mysteriously acquired extra ones, so that a 6-inch knitted square assumed a bizarre rhomboid shape of its own. In any case, I never persevered beyond the first few inches. My cousin Sally, five years younger than me, could turn the heel in a sock at the age of four when even a blanket-square was beyond my capabilities.

AND THERE WERE no cars. They disappeared except for the most essential purposes. My mother and I took the BSA Scout for a final run in Stoddens Lane—at 60 miles an hour, a mile a minute! Afterwards, She (cars were always She to my mother) was set up on blocks in a garage near Green Farm. I don't think I saw Her again.

With so few cars about, everybody gave lifts. Quite often my mother picked someone up in her milk van, and if I was there I had to climb into the back and find somewhere to sit among churns and crates, where I eavesdropped on the grown-up conversation in the front. Once, as I crouched in the cold and comfortless dark, a soldier started talking compulsively about the horrors of some far northern campaign. It was a long story. My mother listened and I listened, but when he said of a fellow soldier, 'We pulled his boot and his whole foot came off ... ,' she hushed him. She hushed him because his words might frighten me (they did) but also because of the whole business of secrecy.

'I wish you hadn't asked the name of that village, old boy.'

YOU MUSTN'T TALK. 'Careless talk costs lives' was one of the slogans, 'Walls have ears' another. You must never give anything away—the person next to you might be a German paratrooper or a spy, waiting to pounce on any useful information. All signposts came down and stations lost their names. Anything that might help the German invader by telling him that he was in Burnham-on-Sea rather than, say, Liverpool was blotted out or taken down—XXX station for example, or The XXX Stores.

Other things affected us children even more directly, food in particular. No ice cream, of course. No bananas and seldom any oranges—we were dosed with rose-hip syrup in winter to give us vitamin C. For tea there was bread thinly scraped with margarine, and really disgusting jams made of unripe tomatoes, rhubarb, or marrow—and always not-quite-enough sugar.

Our school uniform had to change. It had consisted of smart brown tunics over cream blouses, with stripy orange, brown and white ties. Mostly we wore knee socks, but in the cold 1940s winters we had brown lisle or woollen stockings held up by suspenders which were buttoned on to 'liberty bodices', little over-vests with buttons down the front and reinforced tapes to attach the suspenders to. But all this elaborate gear had to go because of a shortage of the brown dye needed for soldiers' khaki. From then on, we wore grey shorts and jumpers with green aertex shirts—not so smart, but less complicated and much more comfortable.

When I was nine or ten, I couldn't see why anyone, ever, anywhere, for any reason, should possibly want to dress in anything other than shorts.

AT SEVEN, THOUGH, I longed to join the Brownies, to wear their brown cotton dress with a yellow scarf and the pointy hat, and dance around the mysterious toadstool that lurked in the cupboard off the gym. At last, in the summer of 1941, I was nearly eight and old enough to join. I became a Gnome (or was it a Goblin? Anyway, I would have preferred to be an Elf or a Fairy, something dainty). For a few weeks I joined in the dancing and played the games, and then it was time for me to take the first of my Tests. My task (a pretty mundane one for a Gnome or a Goblin) was to lay a table, which I did with total disregard for the difference between small and large knives and forks. I failed, and knew perfectly well that I deserved to fail, but, seeing a way through, I pointed out that at school we only had small forks and I could not be expected to know the difference. They passed me. It was gratifying to get the better of the grown-ups—I was far more pleased with my cheating success than I would have been with an honest one. But my career as a Brownie was short: within a few weeks the Brown Owl was called up into one of the armed services and it all came to an end.

IT MUST HAVE been in that summer of 1941, when I was eight, that violent hay fever suddenly invaded my life. There were no antihistamines then. I sneezed and wheezed, and my nose ran, and my eyes itched and when I scrubbed at them with my fists, it only made them sore and swollen as well as blazing. The grown-ups didn't know what to do with me. I overheard them talking—they seemed to think it had something to do with the stress I was under (I wouldn't have known the word, and they probably didn't use it anyway, but I knew what they meant). I dismissed the idea as nonsense. Children think the world is logical. How could my mind bring this affliction to my body without me knowing about it?

They put me in the Sick Room (which, because of the air raids, was downstairs in what had been the kindergarten) and gave me baked custard to eat—made with precious eggs—but I hated the sliminess of it (a bit like the brains in Atbara) so I poured it into my potty. It didn't look right, so I wee'd on top and then, as it was still unconvincing (and I was always full of resource) I slopped the whole lot out of the window on to the rose bed below.

IN THE HOLIDAYS my mother took me to Birmingham University, where a woman scientist pricked my arm and a whole series of little bumps came up showing what I was allergic to—pollen, horses, feathers, cats, dust—the list was long. Injections were prescribed, and I remember running all over the house at Green Farm and hiding under my mother's bed to get away from the doctor, who was pursuing me with his syringe at the ready. Needless to say, the injections made not an atom of difference.

Worst of all was the allergy to horses. Not only was it the most severe, but like most little girls of the time I was horse-mad and had just started having riding lessons, which then had to be abandoned; before long even the presence of someone else's jodhpurs in a cupboard would send me off into agonising spasms of sneezing and itching. There was no escape from pollen or dust, but sleeping on a lumpy kapok pillow made the early mornings a little better.

AT THE FARM during the school holidays, I mostly played with David or whoever else was around. There were good places for hiding or climbing, and plenty going on. We played in the hay in the Dutch barn, picked primroses in the muddy hedgerows in the fields below the farm, and watched the cows coming in and out twice a day for milking. We gave calves skim milk from buckets, dipping our hands in and letting them lick the milk off with their rough black tongues. We fed the chickens and clambered into the henhouses to collect the eggs—you had to pick up them up very carefully, avoiding the china decoy eggs put into the nesting boxes to encourage the chickens to lay.

David and I both had new bikes for Christmas in 1940, serious black ones. We rode them round the farmyard and up and down the lane—further afield sometimes too. Once, when we were a bit bigger, we rode all the way to Clevedon and back.

One day, someone—I think it was Martel—cut off a chicken's head and we stood outside the garden gate and watched, horrified and fascinated, while the headless chicken ran round in circles flapping its wings until it finally collapsed in a lifeless heap of feathers. Someone explained that its brain had told its legs and wings to do these things before the head was cut off. Martel thought it was a great joke.

Another time I went with David and Rosemary to see Auntie

Kit's Mum, who was ill. (Confusingly, the children called her 'Mum' too; 'Gran' was their great-grandmother, Old Mrs Worthington, a bleak little peg of a woman with white hair.) There wasn't much daylight in the room. There was a dark wardrobe and a bed with tousled sheets where 'Mum' lay in a despondent heap, her dark hair straggling across the pillow. Kitty strode about the room picking things up, saying what a mess everything was in and reproaching all and sundry in her live, strong voice. We three children just stood in a line beside the bed and stared. We didn't stay long. Mum was very ill, and she died quite soon afterwards. It was upsetting. I didn't go again.

The Weeks family lived in a small square red-brick tied cottage the other side of the orchard, and beyond that there was an older cottage where Mr and Mrs Badman lived. Mrs Badman was friendly, but Mr Badman lived up to his name and shouted at us: we were frightened of him and kept out of his way. I played with Priscilla quite a lot. In spite of her ringlets, I thought she was all right—but she was the cowman's daughter and went to the village school, which made her different from David and me: children are (or at any rate were) very class-conscious. (Later, she escaped via grammar school to university and got away from the narrow confines of the farm labourer's life.)

She taught me to do cat's cradle, and some country clapping rhymes, most of which were about gypsies:

> My mother <u>said</u> I never <u>should</u>
> Play with the <u>gy</u>psies in the <u>wood</u>
> If I <u>did</u>, she would <u>say</u>
> Naughty-little-girl-to-<u>disobey</u>!

and

> Do you like <u>ap</u>ples? Do you like <u>plums</u>?
> Do you like <u>lick</u>ing gypsies' <u>bums</u>?

And worse. This one had to be said in two voices:

> To the woods! To the woods!
>> No! No!
> To the woods! To the woods!
>> No! No! *I'll tell the vicar!*
> I <u>am</u> the vicar.
> To the woods! To the woods!

ONE DAY THERE was great excitement as one of the bulls was going to serve a cow. David and I were shooed out of the way but managed to hide in the manger and watch through the little gaps under the eaves of the cowshed roof. There was a lot of pushing and shoving and shouting, but we knew what it was about, and more or less got the hang of what was going on.

Later—more than once, I think—we cuddled together on the playroom floor and David fitted his springy little penis (not that I knew the word) into my convenient front slit. It felt nice and comfortable, and I knew that it was naughty, which made it rather thrilling—but that was all. David, a year older than me and at prep school, must have been a lot more knowing. He reminded me about it with crude gestures when we met again as teenagers.

We had discovered at St Christopher's that if you slid down the ropes in the gym at a certain angle you sometimes got a delicious feeling, but we had no idea why. There was something awesome about the big double bed where George and Kitty slept, but otherwise, apart from my grandparents, who slept in twin beds with green silk counterpanes, the grown-ups in my life had their own rooms, and my parents were continents apart. When, a year or two later and I was nine or ten, someone at school drew some pictures of grown-ups with no clothes on and pronounced that if adult men and women saw each other naked they were drawn together like magnets, I flatly didn't believe it. I was quite familiar with the grown-up female body—my mother's and my aunts'. It had sagging breasts and a shapeless tummy and peculiar patches of hair, and it was hideous. I knew where babies came from, just as I knew how calves were born, but I had no notion that there was any excitement about it.

Apart from anything else, we had no vocabulary, Anglo-Saxon or otherwise, for any sexual part of the body—or a lot else. Christmas carols could be embarrassing with their references to wombs and breasts ... 'a breastful of milk ...' was acutely uncomfortable (I had even seen a bowdlerised version). We did not know the word 'fart' although we certainly farted, and when I first lived in France at the age of seventeen and asked what '*merde*' meant, I was not completely sure of the meaning of 'shit'.

THE BBC HAD studios in Bristol and quite often people taking part in broadcasts were lodged at Green Farm. I remember seeing Henry Hall in a pony-trap outside the house, and a musical-hall duo called Nan Kenway and Douglas Young with a little boy of about my age—it was Nan Kenway who took us on that cycle ride to Clevedon.

Most memorable, though, was the Goossens family, who were in Bristol to make a programme about their remarkable musical family—Auntie Sid (Sidonie, the harpist) and her first husband Uncle Bumps (Greenbaum, the conductor) who never ate anything, just drank milk (or so it seemed to us) which was odd. How could a grown-up live on just milk ... ? Then there was oboist Leon, also Uncle to us, who loved to play with my Minibrix (with or without me). Marie only appeared now and then—she was staying nearby. After a few days the broadcast was ready, and David and I were allowed to stay up late to hear it. I remember how magic it seemed, crouching round the wireless with them and listening to them telling their own story. It was a noisy night and the crashing of guns and bombs almost drowned their voices. It must have been in January 1941.

There was something of a bond between my mother and Sidonie—the one with a husband far away and the other with a husband who was drinking himself to death. They belonged to completely different worlds, but they kept in touch for some years after the war.

IN SPITE OF everything, I think the grown-ups had quite a good time. Every now and then they would all swoop off to The Star at the top of the Roddy, the hill on the main road between Cleeve and Congresbury—there was always petrol on a farm—taking us with them if it was a lunchtime excursion. We children played games in the car park or squatted outside the pub listening to the talk and laughter inside, getting more and more bored and hungry, until at last the grown-ups emerged.

ONCE I REALLY contributed. One spring day in 1942 when I was eight, my mother and I went in the van to give a message to Weeks, who was sowing kale (winter food for the cows) in a field some way off. He was furious because Martel hadn't turned up and he hadn't been able to get started. So, while my mother went back to fetch Martel, I took over.

Weeks led the horse and I had to manipulate the very primitive seeding implement, holding it down over the sticky brown lumpiness of the ploughed soil and pulling on a lever at regular intervals to direct the seed into the ground. I sowed two furrows. My mother came back with her camera and took pictures.

MORE OFTEN, THOUGH, I was in trouble, and I remember two occasions in particular. On the first, we are standing in a group near the farm gate. Someone has left a pitchfork under a pile of hay in the manger where we used to play, and Priscilla has gashed her foot on it. She is sitting in a pushchair with her infected foot bound up in bandages—and Martel is accusing me of leaving the pitchfork there. I don't think for a moment that anyone believed that I had (I didn't have access to pitchforks, for one thing—they were hung high up on the cowshed wall ready for throwing hay into the manger). Martel the Guernseyman was simply trying to put the blame on to another outsider. But for many years I felt obscurely responsible—perhaps it had been my fault ... perhaps I had left it there. I could never be quite sure.

On the other occasion, David has fallen into the duckpond, in his Red Indian suit. He howls and says I pushed him. He sank right down, he yells, and his feet touched the dead kittens on the bottom (the litters from the cats that lived under the Black Shed were routinely drowned there). This time I have no idea at all whether I did it or not. Either I pushed him in and was punished and deserved it, or I didn't push him and was not punished—but whatever happened, no feelings of guilt were involved and I recall the whole incident finding grimly satisfying.

THERE WERE ALL the complexities of guilt at school too. The usual punishment for mass misdemeanour was being deprived of a treat. There would be cake for tea, for example, but the naughty ones would sit at a separate table and have none.

Sometimes we were caught stealing gooseberries from the garden. Or there was talking after lights-out in the shelter. We would be asked to own up. On one occasion I didn't, and have no idea whether I had been talking or not. Whatever the truth of the matter, it was somehow more painful to sit at the goodies' table and eat cake than enjoy plain bread with the ungodly.

I LIKED LESSONS. My friend Jill and I always thought we were top of the class, although end-of-term school reports I found recently are not so ecstatic.

Music was my weakest point. I sang in tune, with enjoyment and confidence—'Jane must try not to sing too loudly,' says an early report—but I never knew when to come in: rhythm defeated me. In Band, I remember always shaking my tambourine at the wrong moment and I got it wrong in Singing too.

Piano lessons were worse. A ramrod-stiff lady called Miss Holland sat beside me at the piano rapping the beat while my clumsy fingers tried to find the notes of 'The Jolly Farmer' or the scale of D major, and I hated it. I must, however, have made enough progress to be made to play, in the school concert, a piece called The Otter—and halfway through it I got lost. I searched desperately for the place in the music and had just—I thought—found it when a voice from the audience boomed, 'Jane, I think you had better come and sit down'. I did, with a rush of noisy tears, which caused me to be sent out of the room. I refused to learn the piano after that, which had a disastrous effect on my musical education.

BY THIS TIME, I was reading voraciously. The first book I read right through was—of course!—by Enid Blyton. It was called *Mr Galliano's Circus*. After that I read as many of her books as I could lay my hands on. The point of Enid Blyton is that she creates the habit of reading, opening the way to all the children's classics, from *Winnie-the Pooh* to *The Just So Stories*, *The Secret Garden* and

Heidi and everything else besides. But for me, the story had to end happily. I couldn't bear sadness or anything too frightening, in films as well as books. I wept when Bambi's mother was shot by the hunters and I wept for the baby Dumbo too.

After lunch at school we had a period of Rest, lying on our backs in the gym, and one day, when a teacher started to read Black Beauty to us, I had to shuffle to the far side of the room and stuff my fingers in my ears to avoid hearing about the poor horse's dreadful suffering. Reading *Oliver Twist* too young put me off Dickens until I was in my thirties.

The fairy tales of Andersen and the Brothers Grimm were somehow different: often sad and frightening, but set in a remote world which didn't touch me in the same way—and most of them ended satisfactorily. I consciously identified with the Ugly Duckling. I felt I was an ugly duckling too, an outsider, but if he turned out to be a swan, with any luck I would too. I know I wasn't the only insecure child to be grateful to Hans Christian Andersen for this ray of hope.

The worst of being a small child alone at boarding school is, perhaps, that you can't rely on anyone to be unconditionally on your side. You are always fighting to keep your position in the shifting alliances and friendships of school, and children know very well how to be cruel to one another.

My father sent me photographs of his two new Arab horses —named Majestic and Challenger after the Green Farm bulls— and I proudly showed them to the other children. 'Not properly groomed, not holding their heads up,' they said. 'Nags.' I tore them out of my photo album in shame. In 1943 he travelled up the Nile in a steamer on his way to a holiday in Kenya, and among photos he sent me were two of girls from the Nuer tribe standing waist-high in the river, naked except for a few beads. Out of a painful sense of duty to my distant father I stuck them in the album, but had the sense to hide it from the other children.

I decided to be born on a Thursday instead of a Wednesday because Wednesday's child is full of woe, and I knew that that would provide ammunition for my enemies. If I had seven or eight prune stones on my plate I swallowed a couple to avoid being told that my fate would be to marry a beggarman or thief.

'Your parents can't really want you,' the children said; 'you must be adopted!' By this time I wasn't quite such a cry-baby but my misery would explode in bursts of uncontrollable temper, which always led to even more unhappiness and isolation.

MORE DREAMS, OR rather a waking dream which invaded my mind when I tried to go to sleep. It took two forms. In one I am in a railway compartment which is filling up with eiderdowns, more and more until I am nearly suffocated. The other was even more sinister—a kind of membrane, soft yet slightly pitted like skin, would cling to me, pressing on to me and again preventing me from breathing. Eventually I learnt to fight these invaders off as soon as they threatened to appear, but they were frightening.

MY HAPPIEST TIME in all my years at St Christopher's were the two or three days when Jill (the best friend whom I was never quite sure of) and I had German measles. We were put in the sick room together, but we didn't feel ill and had fun being naughty. We swapped our food and climbed all round the room on the furniture. We poured our horrid milk through cracks over the mantelpiece, whence it trickled down into the sooty fireplace and we tried to dab it off with our towels. Nurse indulged us, certainly, but the main reason for my happiness was the safeness of knowing that Jill was there, almost like a sister, and not having to compete for her.

The school playground is always competitive, but for a child at boarding school there is no relief from the competition, and this in early childhood is destructive.

8. Back to the Midlands

The Allday family—and school

MY MOTHER AND I left Green Farm in the summer of 1942, when I was nine. By then the Blitz was mostly behind us and the Japanese attack on Pearl Harbour in December 1941 had brought the United States into the war. Soon the news of the victory at El Alamein would evoke a nationwide sigh of relief (although we children had only been partly aware of the fear that preceded it). Monty (General Montgomery) was our hero, and Mr Churchill was another. And still we children never doubted we were going to win.

The reason for our leaving was that my Allday grandmother had had a stroke, and my mother had to go home to Sutton Coldfield to help her sister look after her. So we said goodbye to everyone at the farm and rode off on our bicycles to yet another life. Our main luggage must have gone by rail, and we carried only overnight clothes with us—mine in a shiny green doll's suitcase on the carrier of my bike. Weeks, an amateur racing cyclist, had helped us to plan our journey.

WE SPENT THE first night on the far side of Bristol and the second in Cheltenham where we went to a Wild West show. I enjoyed it hugely—but it puzzled me since, with the usual logical and moral absolutism of a child, I couldn't see why all these athletic young singers and dancers weren't in the army. After leaving Cheltenham we pushed our bikes up the long Cotswold escarpment. We were on a main road, but it was empty—I remember hearing a lorry chugging up painfully behind us and then passing us slowly, and the silence that returned ... . We rode on to Stratford and reached Sutton on the fourth day of our journey. It was fun, and quite a feat, but not really very difficult.

What was difficult was settling into the Allday household, which, in the summer of 1942, consisted of my grandmother, who had made something of a recovery from her stroke, my mother's sister, Auntie Lorna, her husband Uncle Nick, my mother and me.

My grandmother was born Minnie Sarsons in 1869—Sarson's Vinegar, people said—not (sadly) because they made it but because of the acid tongue many members of the family possessed.

Way back, according to my mother, the Sarsons were yeoman farmers in a hamlet called Bacon End near Castle Bromwich in Warwickshire—but by the beginning of the nineteenth century the industrial revolution was happening all around them, and they became part of it.

According to various censuses and the records of the Museum of the British Glass Industry, Henry Sarsons, my great-grandfather, was born in 1828 to Joseph, an engineer working in the glass industry, and his wife Mary. By the age of 24 he was listed as a Flint Glass Manufacturer in the Glass Trade Directory and in an 1879 Birmingham paper an advertisement shows the factory in all its smoky splendour.

They made all kinds of glass, but what has survived is largely made up of beautiful table glass cut in the hobnail pattern—water glasses, wine glasses in different shapes for champagne, sherry, wine and port; fruit bowls, decanters and jugs; and silver-capped glass bottles in every size and shape to adorn a lady's dressing table, from eau de cologne bottles to phials for smelling salts. There is even rich red glass—the colour achieved

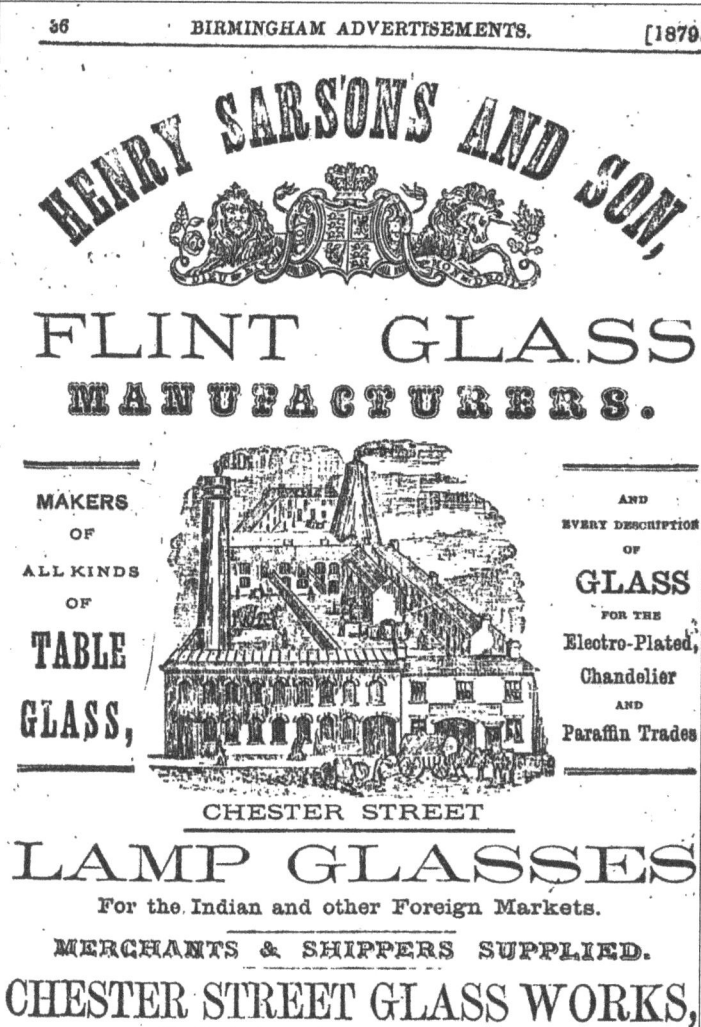

by Henry Sarsons tossing gold sovereigns into the boiling brew of molten glass until it became a wonderful red.

My mother inherited some of this glass. She kept it in a square trunk designed for transporting Edwardian ladies' hats in the room on the top floor at Greenhill Road, which was our domain in 1942. Every now and then she would open it and reverently take out each beautiful, fragile piece, impressing on me that the Sarsons' glass was my heritage and I must look after it and one day pass it on to my children.

IN 1850, HENRY Sarsons married Elizabeth Rooke—she was fourteen if the census is to be believed. The first of their family of seven was born in the same year, and Minnie, the youngest, in 1869. As the business prospered, the Sarsons family moved up the social scale and away from the industrial centre of Birmingham: first from Aston to Gravelly Hill (now more or less obliterated by Spaghetti Junction) and finally, in the early 1870s, to the splendour of Wood End House in Erdington. It was, a house agent's brochure declares, 'The Ancient Manor House of Pype ... an Interesting, Historical and Picturesque House dating from about the year 1543 in the Reign of Henry VIII ... with its Contemporary Cottage & Dovecote and Stabling in grounds of nearly two acres ... .' The family lived there for about twenty years.

I KNOW LITTLE about Henry Sarsons as a person—he had died long before my mother was born—and not all that I do know is good.

One fact is that he was an aspiring politician. The rather unfortunate evidence for this is a copy I have of an 1875 petition to the Court of Common Pleas under the Corrupt Practices Act of 1872, challenging the result of the November 1874 borough election in the Nechells Ward of Birmingham, in which Henry Sarsons had been elected as a Tory Councillor. His opponent, Lewis Woodward, alleged that Sarsons and the Returning Officer had falsified voting papers and the challenge must have been upheld. In statements at the end of the judgment, Sarsons contended 'that he was duly elected' and the Returning Officer said that whatever had happened it was not his fault … . Henry Sarsons' descendants would certainly have known if had been a Birmingham Councillor.

'CLOGS TO CLOGS in three generations' is an old saying, but the Sarsons' rise and fall took only two. Henry died in the mid-1880s and, left to the care of his sons, the profitable glass-making business soon went to rack and ruin.

The eldest son, Harry, lived at Wood End House and kept racehorses, which must have set the tone, and all of them seem to have preferred gambling—horses, snooker, cards—to running a business (though the growing power of trade unions and implementation of legislation limiting working hours probably also played a part).

The last entry for 'Sarsons Ltd, Flint Glass Manufacturers' in the trade directory is in 1895 and the family left Wood End House before the end of the century. By the time it was put up for auction, industrial Birmingham was engulfing the area and, as happens to good houses in the wrong location, it failed to sell. In consequence it was eventually pulled down, and anything of any interest … the oak panelling, the chimneypieces with their 'fluted pilasters and emblazoned shields ...' was sold off item by item and, I am plausibly told, shipped off to America.

I know a bit about Joe, one of the younger sons. To escape his debts, his friends smuggled him on to a ship bound for Cape Town, and he made his way from the Cape to Bulawayo on his snooker winnings (or so the story goes). When he arrived in Cecil Rhodes' great new land of opportunity, he found that the 'Pioneers'—the first British settlers—were in a state of desperation because they could not get their clothes washed properly, so he founded the Matabele Steam Laundry. It was inherited by his daughter Mabel and her colourful husband, widely known as Matabele Mac, who became mayor of Bulawayo and was host to King George VI, Queen Elizabeth and the two princesses, on their Save-the-Empire tour of southern Africa in 1947. It was Matabele Mac—short for Macdonald—and his family who visited 18 Greenhill Road when I was two.

In 1980 I stayed for a few days with his son and his wife in Bulawayo. The Matabele Steam Laundry was still going strong and I was able to identify for them pictures of my grandmother and others in a family album that Joe Sarsons had taken with him on his flight from his creditors in the 1890s.

HENRY SARSONS HAD had the foresight to settle money on his daughters before he died, so my grandmother had her own money. Whilst this was not a fortune, it was enough to find a husband and live decently.

When I was little, women with their own money, like my two grandmothers, had a confidence often denied to the rest. The Married Women's Property Act in 1882 had removed the provision that any wealth a woman possessed automatically became her husband's on marriage but even after that, the tradition lingered and it was the norm for married women to be financially dependent on their husbands. For middle-class unmarried women without money, life was precarious. Some had enough education to become teachers or governesses—like the Brontë sisters—but for many there was the prospect of descending from genteel poverty to worse, eking out tiny incomes by staying for long periods with one set of relatives or another.

Auntie Florrie Flint was one of these virtually penniless gentlewomen, an intermittent visitor at Greenhill Road, stick-like and slightly squeaky, in a neat fawn skirt and a cream blouse with a little frill at the neck, her white hair carefully frizzed in front and scraped into a bun behind. She was always anxious to please, was vaguely irritating, and always hungry—'Having Florrie to stay is as good as keeping hens' was my grandmother's brutal comment.

My mother supported the Distressed Gentlefolks Association all her life.

ONE DAY, WHEN I was nine or ten, I said to my mother, passing on some gossip I must have just picked up, 'Mrs Mitchell lives in that house. She's got a mink coat and she's only a butcher's wife'. (During rationing butchers were widely suspected of doing a thriving business on the side.)

'You must never forget,' my mother rebuked me, 'that you come from a long line of unsuccessful butchers'. Decades later cousins told me that the long line of butchers—or at least, the unsuccessful part of them—was an old family joke, but at the time I took it entirely seriously and was deeply mortified; indeed, the thought of my base lineage caused me unease throughout my schooldays. But perhaps it saved me from being a snob.

My Allday great-grandfather Richard was a Master Butcher, who, an aunt told me, had a successful provisions store in Aston. (Allday is a Warwickshire name: a quarter of all the Alldays recorded in the 1891 census were in the county.)

IN THE PHOTO above we see a group of young people posing for a picture on the Isle of Man in the early 1890s. The two girls are my grandmother, Minnie Sarsons, on the right, and her niece, the rather more sophisticated May. They were much the same age. Minnie's parents died when she was in her teens and she was absorbed into the family of her much older brother, May's father. Sitting on the arm of Minnie's chair is John Allday, my grandfather. Who the other young men were I do not know.

Motorbikes, a thrilling new invention, are possibly the key to this rather odd group. John Allday was born in 1866 and qualified as a Master Tailor but spent his entire working career with BSA, the motorbike manufacturer. In the early 1900s, when the Isle of Man TT (Tourist Trophy) races began, he was manager of the BSA team. So perhaps motorbikes were what these young men had in common, and perhaps John Allday arranged an outing with these girls he knew from Birmingham. My mother was always sorry that I did not know him—a fine man, she said—but he died suddenly in 1928, five years before I was born.

One story about John Allday relates to Mafeking Night in 1899, when the whole of Britain was celebrating a famous victory over the Boers and he drove home from the Birmingham Conservative Club 'scattering the people like cocks and hens'—or so he told his family.

And at Whitsun in 1916 he organised a family visit to Rhyl, where my mother and May's daughter Gwynneth were at boarding school, and drove the car into a ditch—'expertly and expeditiously', according to a letter from Gwynneth's father. It sounded hilarious.

Probably it was. It was a hard-drinking era—'a bottle of port a night' was quite a normal consumption for Birmingham businessmen—and no one had thought of the dangers of drinking and driving.

THERE WAS A bicycle craze in the 1890s, giving people, especially young women, 'a splendid extension of personal power and freedom, scarcely inferior to what wings would give' according to the *New York Times* in 1896, and Minnie made the most of these

Minnie Allday, my grandmother.

new possibilities, cycling, golf, bridge. By all accounts she grew into a spirited young woman, very much the 'New Woman' of the day, and an active member of local women's groups, amusing and jolly, with lots of friends.

This geniality did not extend to her family. At her funeral, friends paid tribute to her kindness, warmth and humour … but 'I never had a kind word out of her!' was Aunt Lorna's exasperated comment. At home, there was an edge to everything she said, and criticism was her natural mode.

Her daughters inherited this characteristic. I once complained to my mother that she never praised me for anything. 'It's because I'm so proud of you,' was her rather illogical and thoroughly Sarsons answer.

IN ABOUT 1910 John Allday built a smart new house for his family in Wylde Green, between Birmingham and Sutton Coldfield, almost in the country and with Walmeley Golf Club just over the road. By the time I knew it, the whole area was built up and it was a fully-fledged suburb.

My mother hated the house. She liked houses that were long and low, like Sunnyside or Hollywood, but 18 Greenhill Road was Edwardian and urban, tall and narrow, with a square entrance hall, good-sized rooms, and a wide staircase with oak balustrades and broad half-landings to the two upper floors.

A huge staircase window went from the bottom to the top of the house, with panes of stained glass through which the morning sun cast brilliant patterns of ruby, sapphire, emerald and topaz on to the walls and floor. It faced due east and flooded the house with cold as well as sunlight. 'Nothing between us and the Urals', my mother said. I took this literally and assumed that 18 Greenhill Road had a unique geographical location. It was the only house I have ever known where the downstairs lavatory, a cramped cupboard under the stairs, smelling of leather and full of golf clubs and walking sticks, was a gents'.

By 1942 Minnie Allday had been a widow for fifteen years. She was elderly and stout and, with her acerbic Sarsons tongue, frightening. I once barged into the bathroom as she was getting out of the bath and simply stopped and stared because she looked quite normal, not wrinkled and old as I would have expected. Understandably, she ordered me out.

My abiding memory of her is coming down the stairs and seeing her standing four-square below me in the hall, wearing a brown-beige jersey dress, her fine white hair untidily framing her round flat pink face—and bracing myself in readiness for the sharp telling-off that was bound to come.

MY MOTHER, PHYLLIS May, was born two months early and 'so small, she fitted into a quart jug'. Her older sister Lorna was then six. Their brother John, my Uncle Jack, was born six years later. The sisters both adored him but hardly knew each other as children. By the time Phyllis was six, Lorna was away at Miss Roberts' boarding-school for young ladies in Rhyl. After she left, my mother and Gwynneth were there in their turn. In a letter to Gwynneth, her father—a prominent Birmingham solicitor—explains that he had sent her to Miss Roberts' school because he 'wanted her to have the very best education possible'. The standard of the local girls' schools in Sutton Coldfield must have been beyond awful. In later life all three women resented the patchy and unambitious education they received from Miss Roberts. It comes alive in a letter Gwynneth wrote in 1915.

> On Monday morning Miss Roberts came down in the most awful rage, and went for everybody ... on Tuesday she was a degree worse if poss and we went about in fear of our lives. On Wednesday she was simply angelic; she excused our lessons and rushed home from an afternoon call ... in order to take us to the Pavilion ... . On Thursday it was Arithmetic morning and you should have heard her go for me. 'You're just like my cook, you are; I never knew anyone like you!!! Will you pay attention to me! It's people like you who are killing our brave soldiers at the front every day!'

IT ALL SOUNDS a bit haphazard. The curriculum seems to have included all the expected academic subjects, including a little Latin, but the girls also had to rehearse for their mothers' At Home days—the drawing room art of balancing tea cups and plates, passing round milk, sugar, bread-and-butter and cakes—and making polite conversation at the same time. After all, when they left school at the age of seventeen, they would be 'putting their hair up' and 'coming out', making calls with their mothers and playing their part in all the rituals of At Home. My mother was not very good at it—so she went off and joined the WRNS.

WHAT MISS ROBERTS did give her pupils, though, was an abiding love of poetry, and Auntie Lorna passed this on to me when she sent me Field Marshall Wavell's anthology *Other Men's Flowers* for my fifteenth birthday. I read the poems—and learnt many of them by heart—at school with a torch under the bedclothes.

Even here, though, there was a snag: all three women talked about 'poitry', which made me creep with embarrassment. Why should I have such an uneducated and unrefined family? How on earth was I going to keep my mother off the subject of English literature when she came down to see me at school … ? It gave me sleepless nights. Some fifty years later I read in a biography of Princess Marie Louise that she 'always stuck to the old-fashioned pronunciation 'poitry'. It was just like the unsuccessful butchers: if only I had known that in my teens … .

AFTER THE FIRST war, Lorna married one of her former patients, a captain in the Indian Army, Nick Trechman, and went with him to India. They were an outstandingly handsome couple and it must have seemed as if a world of opportunity lay before them, but in the military cut-backs of the 1920s Nick lost his job. He worked for a time with Firestone Tyres in Marseilles—Lorna always wrapped herself in a special glamour because she had lived in France—but the job didn't survive the recession and by the time I came on the scene they had been for some time permanent residents at Greenhill Road: an unemployed and humiliated husband and an unfulfilled, unkind and unfaithful wife. I think he bored her to tears.

THERE WAS A certain down-to-earth gallantry about the Alldays. In the First World War, Lorna had been a VAD, a volunteer nurse with the army. She did not talk about it, but I know that her worst memories were not of nursing the wounded and dying in the war itself but of the devastating flu epidemic which followed and killed so many of those who were left. And from the beginning to the end of the Second World War, Lorna worked afternoon shifts in a munitions factory in Castle Bromwich.

Part of Lorna's problem, I'm sure, was that Miss Roberts' school for young ladies never engaged her considerable intellect, and the golf, bridge and gossip way of life in a Birmingham suburb was stultifying. In 1954, when she was sixty,

'A first-class workman's ticket to Hayford, please.'

she went with my mother and me to Greece and her life was transformed: she threw herself into the classical world with all the zeal of time lost, reading everything she could lay her hands on, travelling around Greece and even learning the language. But her friends in Sutton Coldfield were uncomprehending and no one shared her new-found academic passion.

As she grew older, she became more and more eccentric. In the 1950s her Tory patriotism took the form of spitting on non-British cars—or even, my cousin Christopher says, hitting them with her umbrella.

Some years later, my husband and I paid her a visit. She apologised for the house being rather untidy—she'd been out canvassing, she said.

'Who for?' asked Martin, not innocently. It was enough to make her cut me out of her will. (Happily, Uncle Jack forced her to put me back in.)

'Waiting to die, dear, waiting to die,' she would reply to my enquiries when I went up to Sutton to visit her in her old age, a sad summary of a life that was intellectually and emotionally unfulfilled. She lived to be nearly ninety. In the end she found a retirement home called Thalassa—Greek for the sea—in Southsea, not far from where Jack and his wife Mary were by then living. When a taxi came to Greenhill Road to take her there, she walked out of the house—by this time rather dirty and run-down but full of family stuff—without a backward glance. 'Tell the Salvation Army to come and take it all away!' she said. Jack and my mother had to rush up to Sutton to rescue any heirlooms before the Salvation Army got their hands on them.

Very many years later, the chance discovery of a photograph and the vicarious experience of childlessness gave me a clue to something else that might have gone wrong. The photograph shows her, probably in her early twenties, playing with a cousin's baby daughter. She looks sweet and happy. I feel fairly sure that her childlessness was not by choice—although their precarious finances may have been a factor. It must have been the last straw when my mother had me.

Of course, in 1942, I didn't know about any of this. I was told to be polite to Auntie Lorna because she didn't like children; in any case she was an intimidating character and I was rather frightened of her. She was a bit glamorous as well. She slept in a sunny green bedroom overlooking the garden—green carpet, green silk bedcover on a wide bed, green-backed brushes on the dressing-table in the corner. In the morning she would come downstairs in her green kimono and take her breakfast back to bed—smart French-style breakfast, coffee and toast on a tray (it would have been a croissant if croissants had been around in Sutton Coldfield in the 1940s)—eventually emerging in time to tie her hair up in a turban and set off for her afternoon shift at the factory. She had lifelong friends among her fellow workers. On her return it was back to the social round of cocktails, bridge and—on summer evenings—golf.

UNCLE NICK WAS the final member of the household. He slept in a narrow brown bed in a leather-smelling dressing-room next to my aunt's room, 'because he snores', she said. I stared at him so hard one morning when he was eating a poached egg at breakfast—a rare treat in 1942—that he gave me half of it (and I was roundly told off by my mother). He was deeply concerned about my education. Why, in my new-fangled school, was I not learning geography properly, all the English counties and their county towns and rivers? He tried to supply the missing knowledge: 'Northumberland, Newcastle-upon-Tyne ... Durham, Durham on the Weir ... ' but I never got much further than that. My grandfather had similar worries about the modern pronunciation of Latin and the teaching of Euclid (which was Victorian for geometry).

The war was a good time for Nick. He was Captain Trechman, a leading member of the local Home Guard, a man of authority, back in his military element after many years of nonentity. A year or two later, when the danger of invasion had passed, the Home Guard was disbanded and Nick's life became pointless again. He died in his early 60s, suddenly, just before Christmas in 1944, after a bout of flu.

A year later someone put a vicious In Memoriam in the *Birmingham Post*: 'Nick Trechman, remembered only by his friends'. Grown-up speculation about who was responsible switched off abruptly if I was around and I only heard about Lorna's affairs many decades later.

THIS WAS THE household my mother and I became part of in the summer of 1942. Even the house was unsettling: every time I came back from school the rooms had changed: after my grandmother's death her room became my mother's, and then in the summer holidays Uncle Jack's family had moved in, so our domain on the top floor became their territory, and I had to sleep in the sewing room. There was a ventilator over my bed and a crumpled rug cast snake-like shadows on the floor ... and I rather enjoyed frightening myself with thoughts of the snake that slides through a ventilator to kill an unwanted daughter in the Sherlock Holmes story 'The Speckled Band'.

A few rooms stayed the same. Auntie Lorna's elegant green-curtained room, and the grim kitchen and even grimmer scullery, both of them looking out on to a small square of slate-grey yard. Beyond the kitchen was the larder. It had no window, only a big south-facing skylight through which the sun blazed, warming it intolerably on sunny days even in winter—an ordinary window would have allowed the servants to observe what their employers were getting up to in the garden ... not that there were any servants in my day, only the memory of Agnes, whom my mother had loved as a little girl, and others of her family from the Cotswold village of Holford where my grandmother recruited her staff; and a poor old man known simply as Gardener who pottered about from time to time and came round each week to eat his Sunday dinner crouching over the kitchen fire.

THERE WAS A kind of haphazard routine to our life there. My mother went to work early in the morning, in a huge post office in Sutton Coldfield where all the mail for American troops on this side of the Atlantic was sorted and sent on to its different destinations. She would come home at lunchtime, around the time that her sister set off for her munitions factory.

To begin with, my mornings were lonely. In my little sloping-roofed attic room at the top of the tall house (you could almost see the Urals) I read, and taught my dolls to read, from the Book of Flower Fairies and I wished my mother was at home. She would return early in the afternoon and regale me with some of the amazing names American soldiers had—Levi Dreadfulwater, Rollin Pinn—but it didn't make up for her absence. Soon, though, someone found a little girl called Shirley who lived just round the corner and we became best friends for quite a while.

We couldn't have been more different. Shirley was small, pretty, bright but not bookish, into Deanna Durbin, crooners, films and film stars—and, not much later, boys; and me, big for my age and clumsy, consciously clever but childish with it, serious-minded, a real prig. I sometimes wondered why I bothered with her and was amazed when an aunt said she could never understand why Shirley, so much more sophisticated, had bothered with me. She had two brothers. We used to torment the older one when he tried to have a quiet moment with his girlfriend, but the younger one, Brian, tormented us. In the summer he and his friend Peter invented a game called slave-drivers and, armed with sticks, drove us round the gravel paths of their hot garden until I turned round and bit one of them. This caused outrage—it was vicious and unnatural behaviour, they shouted—but it did put a stop to their game.

They were not nice boys. One day they asked me to pull my

knickers down for them. Without a second thought I did so—after all, I was curious about boys' anatomy too, in my intellectual kind of way. They stared, and then called me names which I didn't recognise but I knew were unkind. It was a horrid experience. They told me a bad word—I must say it to my mother, they said. I suppose it was along the lines of 'fuck', but my mind wiped it out afterwards. What I do seem to remember is my mother's reaction—she started smacking me, on the sofa in the front room, and I, a hefty nine-year-old, fought back and got away. Years later I challenged her about this botched attempt at discipline and she swore that the incident had never happened, and even if I had used the bad word, whatever it was, she would not have reacted like that. I have no idea whether it happened or if I just imagined it, but I remember it.

FOOD AT GREENHILL Road was at best unexciting. We ate, but since my mother and my aunt were both busy with their war work and knew little about cooking, it was all rather haphazard. Someone gave the sisters a goose, but they had no idea how to tackle it. They cooked it and then hung it in the larder for days on end while it dripped yellow fat into a succession of bowls, and it all went rancid in the heat.

Just buying food was a nightmare. Everyone had a Ration Book with coupons and 'points' in it. There was no such thing as a supermarket. You had to register with one grocer (as you do with a doctor today) and use coupons for your family's rations of sugar, butter, margarine, bacon, tea and cheese, and with one butcher for your meat.

Other foods like flour, jam, biscuits, and all kinds of dried foods, including dried egg and dried milk, cost points and you could get them anywhere as long as you had enough points in your ration book. Fish (if there was any) and fruit and vegetables were not rationed at all, but all were in limited supply. Fresh eggs were rarely available, so a lot of people kept hens.

People supplemented and scrounged and used their ingenuity: with broken biscuits (no points) from Woolworths and golden syrup (points) and margarine (rationed) you could make a delicious eggless cake. My first cookery was done in the kitchen at Greenhill Road—a Yorkshire pudding made of four tablespoons of flour, two tablespoons of dried milk, one tablespoon of dried egg and half a pint of water. It was delicious. Offal was not rationed. Auntie Lorna cooked tripe and nettles for my lunch one day, memorably disgusting even for Greenhill Road and—like the sheeps' brains in Atbara—left untouched.

Pre-war treats for children simply didn't exist. I cherished the memory of a children's party I went to just before the war with a huge tray of 'mushrooms in a field' ... meringues balancing on top of half-bananas standing in a field of chopped-up green jelly. Only the jelly was a reality in 1942. No ice cream, no milk

'This is what comes of relying on imported oranges.'

shakes, no bananas—and Coca Cola and pizzas hadn't been invented. But you could buy potato crisps: they came in crackly bags with a little blue twist of paper containing a pinch of salt. Occasionally they were even crisp.

SCHOOL FOOD WAS pretty drab too. Once, and once only, I came into the dining room and found a beaming Auntie Wattie standing over a hotplate, a kitchen slice poised over delicious griddle-cooked potato cakes with honey. We ate them with enormous pleasure and longed for her to produce them again, but she never did. Why they suddenly happened and why they were a one-off, we never discovered, but I can see, smell and taste them now. Apart from that, the things I remember are under-cooked and thin rice pudding, damp and tasteless curries, and endless bread and margarine—like all schoolchildren, we assumed that the grown-ups had the butter. At tea-time, the plates of bread were set out with a row of bread-and-marge on one side and a row of bread, marge and jam on the other. You had to have a 'plain' piece before you got a jammy one. But the jam was often so disgusting that we all went for the plain anyway.

To supplement our diet, we were given spoonfuls of malt extract every morning along with our rose hip syrup. There were two kinds of malt—the weedier children had a superior and delicious one, Radiomalt—but I only qualified for it during a brief period when I was nine and it was thought that I was ill.

In truth, as I remember, I had slipped doing a handstand at the end of my bed in the early morning and cricked my neck. Later in the day it was noticed that I was going round with my head on one side and Auntie Wattie whisked me off (in a car!) to the doctor in Brent Knoll. He diagnosed swollen glands, and I was put to bed with a great collar of aromatic sticky stuff called antiphlogiston round my neck. To begin with it was warm and comforting and I liked the herby smell, but once it had gone cold it stuck in my hair and was clammy and horrible.

There were clearly worries, because even when it was decided that I was better I was pushed around in a wheelchair for a bit—but I knew I was all right and felt a fraud. And after that, just for a week or two, I was considered weedy enough to qualify for Radiomalt.

WE CRAVED SWEETS. 'Got any gum, chum?' children used to yell at passing American serviceman, and they tossed it out with great generosity—but I knew that this was not the sort of thing a well-brought-up child like me should do. One day, though, travelling in a First Class railway carriage with Auntie Gwen and only one other passenger, an American army officer, I mortified her by asking him, very politely, if he had any sweets: he did, a bar of chocolate, and he gave it to me. (It didn't taste quite right: it must have been a Hershey Bar.)

It wasn't only food: clothes and even dress materials and knitting wool were rationed too—although there was a more or less respectable black market which even I knew about. There

were plenty of poor people anxious to sell their clothing coupons to anyone who could afford to buy new clothes.

Then there was the business of keeping warm. Most houses I knew had been built at a time when there were housemaids to attend to the coal fires in every room, even the bedrooms, and central heating scarcely existed. Coal fires and coke boilers kept hot water in the taps and radiators, if there were any: and all fuels were hard to get—and rationed. So, getting enough fuel to keep the fires burning and the hot water running was a constant source of anxiety for householders.

First, they had to get hold of the elusive coal merchant, to find out (1) what he had in stock and (2) how much they were entitled to: George Orwell hadn't yet invented Big Brother but respectable people were terrified of being caught cheating. Eventually, the coal man, coated from head to foot in black dust, would arrive on his cart loaded with sacks of coal and coke,

'If we put down our stock as one ton three hundredweights two pounds three ounces, that ought to be near enough.'

which he would heave on to his back and tip into the coal-hole, while his blinkered horse waited patiently outside in the road, chewing on the hay in his nosebag.

At St Christopher's, the water in the dormitory washbasins was frozen some mornings. We used to get dressed under the bedclothes, and the ice-cold sheets burnt your fingers when you made your bed. At home, you sat up close to a meagre fire to keep your front warm, while your back froze. But a proper fire could be magic, lying on your tummy on the hearthrug and gazing at the shimmering and shifting red-gold caverns underneath the burning coals, toasting bread on a toasting fork and eating it with delicious beef dripping.

IN THE HOLIDAYS, at the age of nine or ten I still enjoyed playing with my cousin Robert. Although he was more than two years younger than me, he had sensible things like trains, and we laid out the lines all over the dining room floor. Their road was a cul-de-sac and a playground for all the children in the street: this too was fun and gave ample scope for games. Some of the bigger boys had wonderful go-carts made from old pram wheels and planks of wood on which they swooped down the hill on to the main road. I longed to have one, but I knew they weren't for girls —and also a bit (dreadful word!) common.

Mostly, though, Shirley and I did things together or with other children in and around the neighbouring houses. The golf course—open to all during working hours in wartime—had the best places to play in. There was a footpath between the fairways, but we often strayed from it and nobody seemed to mind, provided we didn't disturb the sheep who mowed the grass. At the far end, at the bottom of the hill, there was a stream which we paddled over into somebody else's woodland, and there was a copse beside one of the greens where we hid and rolled dead leaves into cigarettes and tried to light them with matches smuggled out of the kitchen: a hopeless enterprise—

and if you did for a few moments succeed in making a puff the damp acrid smoke just made you cough. One winter there was snow and we tobogganed down the fairway from the first tee—I on Shirley's splendid toboggan, which she was afraid of, she on my slower cheap one.

If we had a few pennies we could go into the entrance hall of the clubhouse where there was a hatch into the Smoking Room bar and, when we managed to attract the barman's attention, we bought earthenware bottles of Stone's Ginger Beer and drank them slowly, listening to the raucous noise of men drinking beer next door. The barman had a silver plate in his head, from a wound in the First World War, but it was covered with skin and you couldn't see it—only a little dent on his forehead.

THERE WAS SOMETHING chilling about Shirley's house. It was rather grand and had a sunny room called, impressively, a 'loggia', but it was lifeless. Her mother was handsome, but cold and never seemed to do anything. In retrospect I think she probably drank. Her father was small and quite jolly.

One evening a year or two later, when we were about eleven, Shirley and I were in the bathroom in our vests and knickers, getting ready to go to a party. There was a knock at the door and her father asked if he could come in to get his toothbrush. I was standing near the door and began to open it, seeing his bright eyes almost on a level with my own. But Shirley shrieked, 'Don't let him in! Don't let him in!' and flew across the room to slam the door in his face. There were no explanations.

A few years later still, after my parents had come home from the Sudan, Shirley came to stay with us, and I was supposed to pay a return visit in the next holidays—but without being able to say why, I flatly refused to go. In the end my mother had to ring up with some lame excuse that I was ill. The reason was this inarticulable memory. I didn't see Shirley again.

In one way I envied my mother and my aunts and uncles. They were all living close to where they had grown up, and whenever my mother came back to Wylde Green there were lots of people whom she had known all her life. But I lived all over the place and knew I was on my own. Perhaps to compensate for this, I had a strong sense of self and my own lonely individuality. And, because I spent practically all my time in all-female establishments (except for Grandpa), I was entirely without any feeling of inferiority about being a girl (or anything else, really, except of course not being dainty—and having those dubious forebears). But I do remember watching with awed admiration, behind the café at Bracebridge Pool in Sutton Park, as Rolf White peed in a great arc across a dry ditch: I should have loved to have been able to do that!

The Whites were almost family. They were rich and lived in a house with a big garden, and a goldfish tank in the bathroom. There were four children, all with Swedish names—their very smart mother, Britt, was Swedish: Karen (with a long a), Rolf (who was my age and my particular friend), Stefan and Olaf. Sometime in the summer of 1943, we went by a long succession of trains and buses to a cottage they owned near Bewdley, deep in the Worcestershire countryside. It was paradise—mainly, I have to say, because we children were let loose on endless rows of soft fruit—raspberries, redcurrants, whitecurrants, blackberries—which nobody had been there to pick. I also climbed a pine tree and got stuck high up, but I was always doing that: trees, roofs, cliffs ... a passion that ended abruptly a year or two later when I got stuck climbing up the mound on which Criccieth Castle stands ... . I looked up and there was nothing to hang on to. I looked down and saw the sea and rocks. After I had been clinging on for what seemed like hours a terrified fireman climbed down from the top and rescued me.

ONE DAY AT about that time my mother described to me an elegant and lavish dinner party she had been to at the Whites' the previous night—'just like before the war', a real achievement in 1943. I can only remember two details: there had been broad beans slipped from their inner cases, and Karen had waited at table, just like a real maid. I was horrified—one of the children being forced to act as a servant! It offended my sense of what was proper.

A few years later, in their late teens, Karen and a second cousin of mine, Valerie, went off adventuring in a gypsy caravan, causing an immense amount of chatter and disapproval among my aunts and their friends. I was convinced that Karen's rebellion was the result of having been forced to act as a housemaid in her own house.

In a different way, my sense of personal worth was shocked when my Harwood grandmother, sitting at the kitchen table shelling peas, remarked that she had been named Hannah Elizabeth after an older sister who had died as a baby: it seemed to undermine her identity if she was the mere replacement of someone else—and old people died, not babies, surely?

I STILL READ omnivorously—the whole of Arthur Mee's *Children's Encyclopaedia*, which our grandmother had bought for my cousin Bill and me, the *Daily Telegraph* and *Birmingham Post* (today's or yesterday's or last week's spread out on the kitchen table), every kind of children's book: Enid Blyton still, Sherlock Holmes, endless girls' school stories, Kipling, *Picture Post*, and, on my Uncle Nick's recommendation, Jeffery Farnol. I also read Uncle Nick's magazines *Men Only* and *Lilliput*. They didn't have photographs of any kind but plenty of cartoons and entertaining articles. I'm sure there was a lot of smut, but it passed me by.

Then there were the Sunday papers: the *Sunday Express* ('Believe It Or Not ... by Ripley' was what I turned to first) and the *Sunday Times*, which my mother and Auntie Lorna read avidly, with Dilys Powell for films, Harold Hobson for the theatre, Cyril Connolly for books … .

To satisfy our appetite for books, my mother and I quite often went by bus or bike to the Free Public Library in Sutton Coldfield, a brick building standing alone a bit away from the shops, with a tower over the entrance. Endless shelves of books were ranged awesomely round the walls and in different aisles and side-aisles. You had to be quiet and respectful, talking in whispers. It was just like being in church, but more interesting.

In the evenings—the six o'clock bedtime a thing of the past—we usually gathered round the fire and listened to the wireless—'ITMA', 'Much-Binding-in-the-Marsh' and 'Monday Night at Eight O'Clock' (the tunes and slogans from these programmes are with me still) and to programmes like 'The Brains Trust' with the supercilious Professor Joad who put everyone down with his omniscience. (To the whole country's delight he eventually got his come-uppance when he was caught travelling on a train without a ticket.) Then there was the solemn and all-important News: 'Here is the Six O'Clock News and this is Alvar Liddell reading it …' (of course, no women). And if we wanted to give ourselves the shivers, we listened to Lord Haw-Haw, the British traitor who broadcast German propaganda from Berlin every evening.

NATURALLY, LIVING AS I did between one set of grandparents and the other, I absorbed the differences between them and of course adapted my behaviour to conform.

An obvious difference between the families was the caution and gentility of the Harwoods, and the Alldays' scorn of both these qualities. Gentility, indeed, was despised: it was considered not done to shut a lavatory door, and for me one of the hazards of living at Greenhill Road was turning the corner as I climbed upstairs and knowing I might come face to face with my aunt Lorna enthroned across the landing.

Men Only and *Lilliput* at Greenhill Road had their Hollywood counterparts in *Woman's Journal* and *Woman & Home* (and I read those too). Neither Lorna nor my mother would have been seen dead reading one of these middlebrow women's magazines. They probably didn't read *Men Only* and *Lilliput* either, but I did.

The household dogs reflected the difference. The Alldays had bull terriers. At the start of the war there were two: Kim, who belonged to Uncle Jack and had the menacing-but-ludicrous half-white-half-brindle face of his kind, and Bobby, my Aunt Lorna's staffie. Kim soon disappeared—shot while chasing sheep on the golf course. At Hollywood, on the other hand, there was still Nell, the gentle but by now rather elderly cocker spaniel with her matted black and white coat and properly conservative outlook on life.

Even the water was different. Birmingham water came from the Welsh mountains and was soft and better for washing in. But even I knew that this didn't really compensate for the unavoidable fact that Hollywood was in Birmingham rather than the socially more acceptable Sutton Coldfield a quarter of a mile away; and the hard Sutton water tasted better.

It was generally assumed—not least by themselves—that the Harwoods were superior. It came out in all sorts of ways. 'Your mother has such coarse hair,' Auntie Gwen would sigh, pulling a comb through my hair which was unfashionably straight, lacking my mother's natural waves. Harwood hair was, of course, fine—straight, thin, and unmanageable, it demanded perms and a shampoo-and-set every week. Nevertheless, it was more genteel.

When I turned out to be bright, this was of course ascribed to my superior Harwood inheritance—but then, when he was still a very small boy, Bill Allday won a prize at his prep school for a story about midnight feasts (of toothpaste) in the dorm, and everyone said how brilliant he was. Years later my mother told me how pleased she had been to hear of this evidence that some of the brains might have come from the Allday side—as indeed they did. Both Bill and Christopher got Firsts at Cambridge, and Christopher is an eminent mathematician.

THEN THERE WAS safety. At Hollywood, a bomb shelter was built at the side of the house and if there was any threat of bombs we slept there, tucked into bunk beds. At Greenhill Road the attitude was altogether more fatalistic. I remember waking in my little attic room one night in 1942 and hearing the ack-ack of anti-aircraft guns and the whine of aeroplanes. Why hadn't someone come to fetch me to safety? Why wasn't I in a shelter? Didn't they care about me? I asked myself, watching the searchlights scanning the sky. I made my way down the dark stairs and found the grown-ups sitting round the gas-fire in the back room drinking cocoa. 'You looked so peaceful that it was a pity to wake you,' said my mother. Strangely enough, I thought she was right.

ATTITUDES TO ILLNESS marked another difference. *Mens sana in corpore sano* was my mother's lifelong motto. She despised the way her Harwood in-laws asked each other how they had slept every morning, seeing it as a symptom of their constant preoccupation with their health.

One morning I felt ill, which was awkward because we were supposed to cycle to tea with an aged relative in the afternoon. At lunchtime I was copiously sick—and had a glorious vision of a comfortable afternoon in bed—but this was not Hollywood. My mother took a robust view.

'That's good, you've got rid of it, whatever it was. You'll be fine now,' she said as she wheeled out the bikes. And she was right.

RELIGION WAS CONFUSING, too, although I was pretty sure about the basics. God was the Alm Uncle in *Heidi*—old, tall, bearded, distant, but wise and kind, not to mention almighty. Heaven was certainly Heidi's Alps. Getting there—not an immediate prospect—was a matter of being good, and being sorry about it if you were naughty. Before I got into bed at night I knelt and said my prayers, in extraordinary eighteenth-century language:

> Gentle Jesus meek and mild,
> Look upon a little child.
> Pity my simplicity,
> Suffer me to come to Thee.

> God bless Mummy and Daddy, Granny and Grandpa, and Auntie Gwen. And help me to be a good girl. For Jesus Christ's sake. Amen.

Only now do I notice that my Allday relations weren't mentioned.

AT GREEN FARM no one thought of going to church, except on one Easter Sunday when we all—the whole lot of us—paraded to Cleeve Church, which was all decked out with primroses; the vicar must have applied a lot of pressure. I felt it was wrong, an aberration from the natural order.

Nor did church enter into the scheme of things at Greenhill Road, except at Christmas in 1943 when my mother took me to a carol service in Lichfield Cathedral. As the cathedral grew dark, candles were lit, and the treble voices floated out from high up above the choir stalls—a magical memory.

At Hollywood, on the other hand, Auntie Gwen and I walked solemnly to Erdington Parish Church every Sunday morning, gloved and hatted; if there was any petrol, we went by car and Granny came too, but never Grandpa, who reckoned he'd put in a lifetime of church service as a choirboy in Lewisham in the 1880s.

AT SCHOOL WE went to Matins in St Andrew's Church on Sundays, sitting in the front pews on the left, looking at the memorial brass for World War I '1914–1919' on the side of the pulpit (which was confusing).

We were quite pious, although the sermon was usually boring. I relieved the monotony by reading all the fascinating instructions in the prayer book my Harwood grandmother had given me: for example, the mystical mathematics of the 'Table to find Easter from the Year 2200 to 2299 inclusive' (the compilers of the Book of Common Prayer took the long view):

> The Golden Numbers in the foregoing Calendar will point out the Days of the Paschal Full Moon, till the Year of the Lord 2200; at which Time, in order that the Ecclesiastical Full Moons may fall nearly on the same Days with the real Full Moons, the Golden Numbers must be removed to different Days of the Calendar, as is done in the annexed Table, which contains so much of the Calendar then to be used, as is necessary for finding the Paschal Full Moons, and the Feast of Easter, from the Year 2200 to the Year 2299 inclusive. This Table is to be made use of, in all respects, as the first Table before inserted, for finding Easter till the year 2199.

As well as Golden Numbers there were Sunday Letters, which were to be found by 'adding to the Year its fourth part, omitting fractions; and also the number which standeth at the top of the column, wherein the number of hundreds contained in that given year is found. Divide the sum by ... .' It beat 'Think of a Number' hollow.

Strangest of all, though, was the *Table of Kindred and Affinity*, which nestled between the *Articles of Religion* and *Hymns Ancient and Modern*. It began: 'A Man may not marry his Grandmother ... ' The mind boggled.

I shut my eyes tight and covered them with my hands when it came to the Lord's Prayer: '... for ever endeavour, Amen' I prayed, my own prayer, my secret motto. (How I dislike the updated version of *Our Father* with its pointless change to the unpunnable 'Now and for always.')

EVERY NOW AND then I stayed for a few days with a school-friend. One was the daughter of the Archdeacon of Bristol, and on the Sunday, naturally, we went to church—not in a proper church, though, because the parish church had been bombed and the service was held in a kind of tin hut, packed with people. We crammed into a pew somewhere near the back and I opened my prayerbook confidently and waited for the familiar words. But when words came, they were the wrong ones. Everything was strange, people kept standing up and sitting down without warning and ... I stood there totally bewildered, bereft, tears pouring down my cheeks, while the grown-ups (whom I hardly knew) were too far above me and participating too enthusiastically to notice that their small guest was weeping. It must have been a family communion service, an innovation that hadn't hit the parishes where I went to church, which all had Matins as the morning service.

It was all a bit puzzling, but at least—except in Bristol—I knew what was done where, and conformed.

IN DECEMBER 1943, coming home for the holidays, I was put on the train at Templemeads Station in Bristol and told that my mother would be meeting me at Cheltenham. The train was steamy, hot, and crowded, as wartime trains tended to be (unless they were crowded and cold), with people and luggage piled into all the corridors.

At Cheltenham, anxious not to lose my seat, I went to the door and stood on the top step scanning the thronged platform for my mother who would, I assumed, be joining me on the train, but there was no sign of her. It seemed sensible to stay on the train and go on to Birmingham. I knew I could then get a train from Snow Hill to Chester Road Station, quite near my grandparents' house. The whole carriage rallied to the cause of the lost little girl who was so brave and independent, and I had the pleasant feeling of being a bit of a heroine.

Eventually, well after dark, we arrived at Snow Hill and someone helped me to buy a ticket and find the suburban train to Chester Road, and from there I lugged my suitcase and turned up bursting with achievement at the Hollywood front door. I was greeted with amazement and relief—I think there was a police search out. I hadn't understood that I was meant to get off the train at Cheltenham, where we were to have had lunch with friends. My adventure went very sour when I realised that I had been a bit stupid and caused everyone such awful anxiety.

ON CHRISTMAS MORNING there was a great party at Greenhill Road, with all the friends of all three families in the house talking at the tops of their voices and shouting and laughing. They even dragged the postman in to join the fun—there was a postal delivery on Christmas Day in those days! He brought just one letter in a small brown envelope. The next day my mother took me out for a walk and, just by the pillar box at the end of the road, told me what it contained: a travel warrant for her to take a train to Glasgow and join a ship which was leaving in a convoy for Alexandria in a few days' time. My father would come to meet her there. Although I hadn't known about it, she had been trying for a long time to get permission to join my father in the Sudan, and had been honing her long-forgotten secretarial skills so that she could qualify as useful to the war effort. At last, she had been offered a job as secretary to the Governor of the Province of Atbara. She was to leave almost immediately, and I would go to Hollywood for the rest of the holidays. She had no idea when she would be back.

I felt bleak. I understood why she was going, but also understood that, with my mother, I came second best. A couple of days later, she was gone.

9. Growing Up

WITH AUNTIE GWEN, I sensed that I came first—but it was a bit worrying. She was devoted to me and I loved her—indeed, in some important senses she taught me how to be loving. But she fussed me and tried to call me 'Janey', which I hated.

'When I'm old', she used to say, 'all I want is to live in a little cottage somewhere near you'. Guiltily, I found the idea unnerving. For the time being, however, she was the most important person in my life, and my legal guardian.

The eldest of the family of five, she was then in her late forties and had spent her whole life as a daughter. Just like the Allday girls, she and her sister Norah were sent to a boarding school in North Wales, but it was a more established school, Penrhos College, and they had a more organised but still unambitious education.

She was eighteen when the First World War broke out and during the war she worked in the office at her father's factory. She had a head for figures and would probably have made a good business-woman, but my old-fashioned Harwood grandparents would have found such an idea unacceptable in peacetime, so she gave up her job and stayed at home -and in the husband-shortage aftermath of the First World War I don't think there was ever any suggestion of marriage, the only means by which she could have escaped. The special charge she had of me was of the utmost importance to her.

My Allday and Sarsons forebears were all, as far as I know, Midlands born and bred, but the Harwoods, and Granny's family, the Larkins, had migrated from all over the country to make money in Birmingham.

The Harwoods were northerners. My grandfather's great-grandfather, Peter Harwood, was born in 1778 in Cornforth, an industrialising village a few miles south of Durham, and owned the Stafford Pottery in Thornaby, together with the 'brown clay' pits which supplied its raw material. By 1828 he and his son, Thomas, born in 1804 in Coxhoe, were in partnership as manufacturers of 'brown earthenware'. Peter must have retired in 1831, when the London Gazette records that the father-and-son partnership was dissolved, and he died in 1843. When his wife Mary died in1847 the estate was valued at £450.

The business prospered and expanded under Thomas's ownership. The records give evidence of an ambitious and successful businessman who pursued his own autocratic way in his private life as well as in business—even if it meant defying the law—and in the end alienating his family

His defiance of the law was to do with marriage. His first wife was Ursula Gray of Stonegrave, Nunnington, in Yorkshire. She bore him four sons between 1838 and 1843 but died when they were very small. It seems likely that her sister Sarah came to help with the little boys because a few years later, in 1851, Thomas married her—in Germany, because marriage between a man and his deceased wife's sister was illegal in England. The Church had always frowned on such unions—think Henry VIII —and the1835 Marriage Act had made them unlawful. However, it was the humane and sensible thing to do: the boys grew up with Sarah as a mother figure and she spent her last years with the eldest of them, Peter. The local church, too, must have accepted this irregular union: Thomas, Ursula and Sarah are buried in the same grave in St Mary's churchyard in Norton.

As for Thomas Harwood the businessman, his career shows ambition and acumen. In the early 1830s, soon after his father retired, Thomas bought the bigger Clarence Pottery in Norton. Over the next fifteen or so years there are occasional mentions of the Harwood potteries in local newspapers—a six-month strike at the Stafford Pottery in 1836 and a 'hurricane' in 1843 which blew down a chimney at the Clarence works, causing considerable damage and one serious injury.

Then, in the late 1840s, Thomas bought much bigger premises in Norton and moved the major part of the business there, still calling it the Clarence Pottery—with the original site now renamed the Old Clarence. This acquisition enabled development, diversification into ornamental products, and an emphatic move up market. With ninety-seven men, fifty-nine women and thirty boys on its books according to the 1871 census, the local papers rated Thomas Harwood as an important local employer.

His second son, another Thomas, was partially blind and an organist living on an annuity. The other three, Peter, John and James (the last being my great-grandfather, born in 1843) joined the family firm in the course of the 1860s, but it seems that they didn't come up to their father's expectations and he remained fully in charge of the main business. It was perhaps to give them a role that in his mid-sixties he set them up as 'Harwood Brothers' at subsidiary sites, Old Clarence Pottery and South Stockton Brown Potteries but the partnership came to nothing. The *London Gazette* records its founding in 1869 and its dissolution 'by mutual consent' only two years later, in 1871.

It strikes me that there are similarities between Thomas Harwood and Henry Sarsons because both were successful entrepreneurs and both established flourishing businesses which did not long survive them. And both were would-be Tory politicians—'Harwood is as crack'd as his pots' says an undated election poster on behalf of the Whigs—but neither was elected.

THOMAS SENIOR DIED in September 1876, and his will showed how little he thought of his sons as businessmen. Its main stipulation was that the flourishing Clarence Pottery must be put up for auction in September 1877 (if it had not already been sold) and the proceeds shared between Peter, James and John (the blind Thomas had his annuity and Grove Villa, where their father had lived). The buyers, local businessmen, acquired the right to use the name Harwood for all their goods. With the disappointing proceeds, Peter bought an annuity and retired; John kept the Old Clarence Pottery going (it lasted on a relatively small scale until the 1930s); and James, in poor health and married with three children, was by this time living in London.

The will was disputed on all sides, giving rise to litigation that lasted for over nineteen years. James's father-in-law was one of those who made claims against it.

BY THE TIME of his father's death, James Harwood was living with his wife Mary Ann, formerly Barton, and their three small children at 109 St Donat's Road, a modest house in a quiet part of New Cross not far from Mary Ann's family home in Dartmouth Villas near Blackheath.

The children were all born in Stockton, Frederick, the eldest, in 1869 (the year when the Harwood brothers' partnership was set up), Ethel Maud in 1870, and James Herbert, my grandfather, known as Bert, in 1871 (the year that it was dissolved). How and where James and Mary Ann had met, when they moved to London, and why, I don't know. Auntie Gwen had the impression from Mary Ann (her grandmother) that she couldn't stand living in the north; perhaps both she and James needed to get away from an authoritarian father and father-in-law.

James outlived his father by little more than a year, dying on 19 October 1877, aged only thirty-four. He is buried in the same grave as his father in Norton.

THE BARTON FAMILY came from the Weald of Sussex and in the eighteenth century had been part of the great economic migration to London, settling, as many from the Sussex did, in the south-eastern part of the city. The family kept up their Wealden connection long after they had moved: the births—in London—of all their children and grand-children are recorded on a Wealden genealogical website.

Mary Ann's grandfather, William Noakes Barton, had at one time a shop at 179 Regent Street selling hosiery and gloves; his wife was formerly Mary Lambert 'of Prospect House, Wadhurst'. Their son, another William Noakes Barton, born in 1819, was a shipping and insurance broker in Leadenhall Street, and married Jane Wilson. Mary Ann, born in 1847 in Blackheath, was one of their six girls and three boys. (Her sister Rosa's son, William Larke, born in 1875, was a famous engineer, knighted for his contribution to the use of welding in construction. His portrait is held by the National Portrait Gallery.)

THERE WAS CERTAINLY not much money about for the widowed Mary Ann Harwood, but in one way and another there must have been enough to keep the family going and give the children a decent education. The boys attended Colfe's Grammar School in Lewisham, and Ethel went to Haberdasher's Aske's at Hatcham in New Cross.

One source of funds was from a trust set up by Mary Ann's maternal grandfather John Wilson, born in Glasgow in 1790 but long resident in Lewisham, and the owner of cargo ships based at Surrey Docks—probably dirty British coasters plying between London and the coalfields of the north. In his portrait, painted in the 1840s, he looks prosperous and jolly, but his wife, Ann Slater from Whitby, looks tired, even grim.

On 7 September 1860, when he was seventy, John Wilson 'being possessed of ten shares in the Southwark and Vauxhall Water Company of £100 each numbered 2106 to 2115 inclusive is desirous of settling the same for the benefit of himself his wife Ann and his grand-daughter Mary Ann Barton ...' . It goes on to specify that the income from the shares must be for Mary Ann's 'sole and separate use and not subject to the debts claims control or engagements of any husband with whom she may intermarry'—a necessary protection for a female before the passing of the Married Women's Property Act.

I have a copy of the Deed modifying the original to appoint Mary Ann's son, my grandfather, as a trustee in place of a dead uncle. It is dated 12 January 1905, hand-written, long, tedious, repetitious, without punctuation and full of archaisms —'witnesseth', 'the said ____' and 'the aforesaid' and random heightening of words like Whereas, Between and Now throughout the document. (Clerks were paid per word and were inclined to be long-winded.)

I PRESUME THAT Mary Ann was not only the beneficiary of John Wilson's trust. He had two sons, John and Edward, who were the original trustees and most likely had families of their own, and she herself was one of nine. Probably, as a ship owner, John Wilson was wealthy enough to settle a thousand pounds—a lot of money in 1870—on all his many grandchildren. Thirteen years after John Wilson's death, the trust income must have been a godsend to Mary Ann Harwood when her husband died, leaving her with three children, aged eight, seven and six.

I KNOW NOTHING about Grandpa's childhood, except that he went to Colfe's and was a choirboy in the local parish church. He often reminisced, though, about his life as a young man about town in the London of the 1890s—Marie Lloyd and the music halls, and Quaglino's and Oddenino's and other restaurants of fashion. But I don't know what he did for a job or money. Before long, he and his brother both solved their financial problems by marrying the daughters of a successful self-made Birmingham businessman, Samuel Collins Larkins, who owned the largest wholesale drapery warehouses in the Midlands.

Ethel married a charming but improvident man called Montague Lucy and was the final beneficiary of John Wilson's trust. Her son, the grandly named Reginald Montague Harwood Lucy, was a clerk with Purley Borough Council, living with his mother and intent on proving that he was related to the Lucys of Charlecote, where Shakespeare is said to have been caught poaching deer. An aeroplane propeller on the wall of his council flat was a reminder that he had been a pilot in the Royal Flying Corps in the First World War and, according to my father, quite a lad.

LARKINS COUSINS OF mine have traced our forebears from parish records in the village of Gamlinghay in Cambridgeshire. John Larkins, born in 1631, was by trade a carpenter—as were his sons and grandsons—but he also held the post of parish clerk, registrar and sexton of the local church. He died there aged 80 in 1711. The births of forty Larkins children were recorded in the parish register in Gamlinghay between 1700 and 1750.

His son, another John Larkins, had nine children, five of whom survived infancy; one of them, William, born in 1704, seems to have moved to the neighbouring village of Eynesbury in Huntingdonshire where his son, also William, born in 1732, married Sarah Ibbott in 1755 and became a glover.

Charles, their only surviving son (of eight children), followed the same trade. He married Sarah Robinson and moved to nearby Biggleswade in Bedfordshire, where their five children were born, one of the two who survived infancy being Joseph, my great-great-grandfather, whom we know a bit about thanks to Army records.

PRIVATE JOSEPH LARKINS, born on 20 December, 1793, fought at the Battle of Waterloo. He joined the Bedfordshire Militia under

Captain J Lowery when he was twenty and was transferred to the 40th Foot, fighting in Spain in the last phase of the Peninsular War, and against Napoleon's army under Marshal Soult at Toulouse in April 1814. His regiment was sent to New Orleans for a short time and returned through Ireland in time to join Wellington's army at Waterloo. He 'took gunshot wounds to the head' in the battle and after two months in a hospital in Brussels he was returned to base and discharged as unfit in October 1816.

Five years later, he married Hannah Cooper and by the time he died at the age of 40 in 1833 they had had six children. Two of them died young and a third at the age of twenty. Samuel Collins Larkins, born in 1828, the middle of the three that were left, went on to become a highly successful businessman.

Hannah is the heroine of the story in the early years, keeping her young family afloat. They soon had to abandon glove-making; apparently an embargo on the importation of French gloves was lifted in 1825 and the bottom fell out of the market for English ones. This may have had something to do with their move from Biggleswade to Luton and their engagement in the great local business of making hats.

In 1852, on his marriage certificate, Samuel is described as a blocker, so he knew how to make hats—but business was his real talent, and he and Hannah are credited with founding the family fortune: rather than selling their hats to a middleman in Luton they carried them into London and did their own marketing, probably in the Hatfields area of Southwark, just down the road from where I live now.

In the early 1860s, prosperous but looking for greater opportunity, they moved to Birmingham, a magnet for ambitious entrepreneurs partly because of all the activity and the skills available, but also because there were no guilds to restrict enterprise.

There, Samuel founded a wholesale drapery business, S.C. Larkins, which in time made him very rich indeed. He and his

wife (*above*), born Harriet Gutteridge, had six children and 25 grandchildren who proliferated all over Sutton Coldfield. I don't know when his mother, the gallant Hannah died: perhaps it was around 1866 when the first Hannah Elizabeth Larkins had a brief existence—to be replaced in 1870 by the second Hannah Elizabeth, my grandmother, who was born in Birmingham, well after the family had moved there, probably in Gravelly Hill, an

early suburb of the rapidly expanding industrial heart of the city. I have no evidence of Granny's early life, except for a chilling photograph of her school (*see previous page*), which can only be described as a dame school for the daughters of the newly wealthy. Granny is the girl in the middle of the back row.

JAMES HERBERT HARWOOD and Hannah Elizabeth Larkins met at Ventnor in the Isle of Wight when they were in their mid-twenties—not exactly a chance meeting, since Fred Harwood had already married Deborah Larkins (who was a good twelve years older than he was). Bert and Hannah married in 1895, and over the next ten years produced five children: Gwen, Lester, Jim, Norah and Gerald. Before long, after an unsuccessful foray into the electrical business, Grandpa set up a factory making children's clothes—I can't help thinking that he must have had support from his father-in-law. This business, later named (modestly) World's Wear Limited, kept the family going for nearly a hundred years.

FOR THE NEXT five years, until my father retired from Sudan Railways, Hollywood was my home. At the age of ten I found the name Hollywood embarrassing, but Grandpa said it had been called that long before the Los Angeles Hollywood had been invented ... .

The house was not grand but—much better—it was old, sprawling, and full of history. The oldest part—now the cool and capacious stone-flagged larder—had started as a tiny cottage, a single room with a staircase leading up to a low-ceilinged bedroom above. At some stage, probably in the late eighteenth century, this cottage on the main road from London to Chester was transformed into a coaching inn, The Bell, which is marked on old route maps. Three large rooms were added along the front, all opening into a tiled passage that ran from one end of the house to the other, linking these public rooms to

My drawing of a balsa wood model of Hollywood I made when I was 14.

the old cottage and the single-storey pantry, kitchen and scullery adjoining it. A rather meagre staircase (considering the size of the house) twisted up to bedrooms above, and there were steps down to huge cobwebby cellars with rows and rows of built-in wine racks, where Grandpa kept his last few cherished bottles. Another wing—the breakfast room, with a bedroom above it—was added on later.

The house was full of pictures; my grandfather considered himself to be something of a collector. There were oil paintings in the drawing-room, and prints and engravings all over the house. Halfway up the stairs hung an etching of Burne-Jones' *King Cophetua and the Beggarmaid*, which always intrigued me. But the strangest was behind the sofa in the breakfast room—*The Naiad*, a four-foot-long semi-draped woman lying in water among reeds and gazing at you with a vapid pre-Raphaelite stare.

There were two bathrooms but only one inside lavatory, and all three conveniences had been tacked on to the old building comparatively recently. We weren't so far from the age of the wash-stand in every bedroom, and a chamber-pot under every bed, with housemaids or chambermaids to empty them all in the morning. When I was little, Vera, the housemaid, did this chore, but the war had changed all that. I have a vision of a morning procession of adults carrying their chamber pots to empty them into the only lavatory. Everyone was used to this procedure and it was awkward only when Grandpa's sister, my Great-Aunt Ethel, came to stay. I can remember her for three things: her gaunt black-clad figure, her general disagreeableness, and the grumbles of the other grown-ups because she spent half the morning in the lavatory, so that everyone else had to use to the cold and cobwebby servants' outside lavatory next to the coal-hole in the back yard.

IN FACT, THERE were two back yards, pre- and post-motor vehicles, the old cobbled one by the kitchen door with its gate marked 'Tradesmen's Entrance' and the newer concreted yard in front of the modern garage block, which housed not only cars but also the washhouse, a potting shed and a kennel with a caged-in run for dogs (but Nell was a house dog and was never put in it). There were also two large upstairs rooms presumably intended by some previous owner for servants to live in.

These upstairs rooms were full of the accumulated junk of family life, dumped there when my grandparents and their remaining grown-up children moved to Hollywood from their childhood home in Sutton Coldfield in the 1920s. I made these lofts my private territory—when it was warm enough. There were trunks and suitcases, odd bits of furniture, old tennis racquets and golf clubs, collections of cigarette cards, children's books from the early part of the century, and the bound volumes of the original early twentieth century edition of the aforementioned *Children's Encyclopaedia,* which came out week by week when the young Harwoods were children.

I would read these volumes from cover to cover, as I had the 1940s version, soaking up all sorts of useful and less useful facts: the colours of the prism, scientific discoveries of 1910, stories of adventure and Empire, and mathematical tricks including one which showed you how to prove that one equals two. I spent hours making paper models of towns and villages according to instructions in the encyclopaedia—a pastime that led to the balsa wood model of Hollywood a few years later.

THERE WAS MORE than an acre of garden. A high, dark, holly hedge defended the front of the house from Chester Road, and a brick wall with ferocious bits of broken glass cemented on top ran most of the length down Orphanage Road at the side, but at the far end, where the artichokes and marrows and compost heap were, the wall turned into a perfectly ordinary wooden fence, which I thought rather illogical.

To this day I can remember where the onions were, and the broccoli and cauliflowers and the potatoes ... and the rows where Auntie Gwen picked her runner beans for the kitchen, and sweet peas for the breakfast room table. I can place the Beauty of Bath tree in my mind's eye—the first of the apples to ripen, but soft and disappointing—and the Worcester Permain, which came next in the season, but not the Coxes and Russets and Bramleys, because they ripened long after I was back at school. There were still hollyhocks on the garden side of the garage, fuchsias along the paths, roses at the end of the lawn, lilacs by the fence at the bottom, and two intriguing furry-stalked sumachs by the steps to the tennis court (it was a hayfield in wartime).

In the front garden, south-facing yet dark from the holly hedges and a huge monkey-puzzle, there were neat beds of red geraniums and blue lobelias edged with white alyssum, a thoroughly patriotic display. There were sooty summer-houses in various not-very-sunny places. The biggest of them still housed the dolls' house which I had loved so much when I was little, but by now long exposure to weather and the smoke of a million coal fires had made it black and dirty.

THE HOUSEHOLD I returned to at the beginning of 1944 consisted of Granny, Grandpa, Auntie Gwen and Harriet the maid.

Granny still had the familiar assurance of a woman with money of her own—substantially more money, in fact, than my Allday grandmother. She was by this time in her mid-seventies, a large woman who moved with slow dignity, always wearing an ankle-length silk or fine wool dress made for her by dressmakers called Corbett's in town, V-necked with a dicky or modesty vest underneath. Her hair was fluffy and white with a bun at the back. At night she plaited it neatly in front of the mirror. She was kind but undemonstrative; her 'butterfly kiss' was still the nearest she got to intimacy.

She didn't say much but her words had weight. One evening, soon after my arrival, she saw an airgraph that I had addressed to my father: Mr F.L. Harwood, Sudan Railways, Atbara, Sudan. She was shocked: he was a gentleman and must be addressed a such: F.L. Harwood Esq. It was clear that I had done something deeply wrong. And such was Granny's gravitas that it took me many decades to get rid of a hang-up about it.

Grandpa was still my special friend. He went to work most days, and once or twice I drove to one of the factories with him. His car, a grey Wolseley, was always 'warmed up' by the gardener, now a rather grumpy old man called Hill, and he would drive it with one foot on the accelerator and the other on the clutch in a series of swoops—dreadful driving, my mother called it, but I was just excited to be in a car at all.

The factory, little more than a huge shed in a drab street served by old-fashioned trams with outside staircases, was a temporary one, as the largest and newest of World's Wear premises had been requisitioned as a munitions factory. It was filled with the whirring sound of sewing machines and rows of women and girls operating them. It was drab work, too. When my mother made dresses, everything from the cutting out to the seams and hemming was creative and exciting, but in the factory each machinist did just one seam, only a few inches, on each garment, whirr, whirr, before passing it on to her neighbour and reaching out for the next bit. I felt awkward and out of place there.

MORE OFTEN, GRANDPA and I pottered—even worked—in the garden, or took Nell for a walk after tea, down Chester Road to Pype Hayes Park and back. (Without knowing it, we were quite close to where the Sarsons' Manor of Pype had been.)

It was in some ways a melancholy walk. The area was going down and Hollywood and a few other larger houses like it had become marooned in a tide of between-the-wars semis, which Grandpa hated. The grandest of these houses—stucco with a pillared front—belonged to some people called Homer. My mother had told me about going to tea there when she was little. The parents hadn't spoken for years and when the family sat round the tea-table (as families did in those days), Mrs Homer would ask one of the children to ask his father if he would like more tea, the response coming back by the same route. Anything better than the stigma of divorce.

AUNTIE GWEN DID war work. She had been an air raid warden during the air raids in the early forties. Later, she packed Red Cross food parcels for prisoners of war in Germany. I went with her once. It all happened in the basement of the City Hall where an army of middle-class women packed the parcels in an atmosphere of strenuous goodwill and fellowship. Everything had to be done at speed and correctly. I felt quite important putting tins of this and that and bars of chocolate into the parcels that the Red Cross would send Behind the Enemy Lines, into Germany itself, to bring a bit of cheer to the poor POWs. There was a raffle and I won a bottle of sherry, which pleased Auntie Gwen more than me. Auntie Gwen was especially good at stringing and tying the parcels with extra-secure knots, no slack in the string. She was always an expert parcel-packer—unlike my mother, who once posted a chocolate birthday cake to me; it arrived as crumbs which had to be eaten with a spoon.

MOST OF AUNTIE Gwen's energy, however, was dedicated to keeping up standards, and mealtimes had none of the hazards of Greenhill Road ones. Rations were supplemented in any way possible: vegetables and fruit from the large kitchen garden, chickens and eggs obtained from relations in the country and I don't know where else … . Auntie Gwen salted beans, preserved eggs in something called waterglass, made jam, bottled fruit and made everlasting expeditions to the shops to ensure that the family was never without.

We ate well. In spite of rationing, I'm sure we had meat or fish every day. Best of all was a chicken. A chicken in the 1940s was nothing like a supermarket broiler: it was a serious bird who had spent a good life scrabbling round a farmyard or chicken-run, and one fed a family—with something left over for tomorrow. Sometimes it was a boiling fowl, an elderly hen past laying, which would be boiled for a long time and served with parsley sauce: very tasty. More often it would be roast chicken, with rolls of bacon and bread sauce—even chipolatas on special occasions.

Auntie Gwen would carve with ceremony, giving to each person the piece they liked best: white breast-meat for Granny and herself, the darker leg-meat for Grandpa, and a bit of both for me. But I would always have the wishbone—the merry-thought—and after I had scraped and sucked every last bit of delicious meat off it and let it dry on the side of my plate, Grandpa and I each took hold of one side of the forked bone and made a wish as we pulled it between us until one side broke off. Somehow, I always got the bigger bit so my wish would come true. Chickens don't seem to have wishbones nowadays.

Everything was organic—not that anyone had thought of the word or dreamt of there being any alternative. Vegetables were of the earth and earthy, and apples and lettuces were shared with caterpillars and bugs. Chickens were the original free-range—and if you were making a cake or scrambling eggs you had to break the eggs one at a time into a cup to make sure each one was fresh, because if you broke a bad one into a bowl of eggs, the whole lot had to be thrown away. You didn't often get a bad egg, but if you did the stink was unforgettable.

At mealtimes, there was—in retrospect—a peculiar seating pattern. Granny sat at one end of the table, Auntie Gwen at the other, my grandfather at the side. This in a way summed up the pattern of the household, in which my aunt held the reins of power but my grandmother ultimately dominated. Grandpa was marginalised but comfortable in his seat at the side with his back to the fire, and I sat beside him, fitting back happily into the habits of previous years. Auntie Gwen would do the serving —starting with Harriet, who would creep into the room with her plate for Auntie Gwen to serve her portion. She was a bent little woman with wispy straw-and-orange hair who asserted her gentility in a refusal to eat herrings, which she regarded as common. She was not strong, so the harder work was done by Annie, who came in most days.

THE HOLLYWOOD DAY started with the sound of Harriet, dressed in her cotton morning uniform—a pink or blue dress and plain white cap and apron—bringing tea to the grown-ups in their bedrooms. This was soon followed by Auntie Gwen's smoker's cough hacking away in the silence (all my aunts smoked: it was a sign of emancipation).

Breakfast was a leisurely affair at half-past eight or nine—

Rice Crispies, toast, even very occasionally a boiled egg—and was the prelude to a morning of shopping, cleaning, and preparing lunch, which was at one.

Occasionally we went by bus to Evans the Butcher's in Sutton Coldfield, where the family was registered, in the hope of getting some offal which Mr Evans might have kept for us. ('Surely, you aren't going to ration me, Mr Jones,' was the caption on a Pont cartoon featuring a wealthy lady confronting her wilting butcher: even as a child I thought it was apt.) More often, we walked to the nearest shops at Chester Road Tram Terminus—Mr Ricks the bad-tempered greengrocer (potatoes at seven pounds for sixpence, I remember); Hughes the fishmongers; Timothy Whites, the chemists, which ran a circulating library where I sometimes had to exchange my grandmother's very undemanding library books.

There was also the Co-op, which Grandpa regarded as enemy territory—but if they had something that wasn't in any of the other shops you had to mentally cross yourself (or the Tory equivalent) and go in.

If I was around, I had to undertake this treacherous mission. Grandpa was Conservative to the core. He once explained to me how wicked the Liberals were, because their policies of laissez-faire meant that employers didn't look after their workers properly. His attitude to the working classes was paternalistic: he saw them as almost a different species, and the Labour party hadn't penetrated his political consciousness at all. He was rather in favour of a certain degree of unemployment: it kept the workers in order.

AFTER SUCH AN energetic morning, and lunch, all the grown-ups had a good long rest. This was agony for me since I was not allowed to make a noise. I went out if I could, to Shirley's or to tea with Robert and Sally for example.

'What time are you going?' Auntie Gwen would ask.

'Half-past two.'

'You can't go out to tea at half-past two! People will be resting!'

But I could, and I did, and they weren't.

OFTEN THOUGH, ESPECIALLY in the winter when it was too cold to go outside or explore the lofts, I had to spend the afternoon in the house. I wasn't, for understandable reasons, allowed to play the piano or make any kind of noise, so I read (mostly) or made models, or drew, or played with paper dolls which you cut out of books and then clothed with a variety of garments—the 1940s equivalent of Barbie dolls I sometimes think. But however busy I was, two hours of silent solitude is a long time for a child.

Eventually, at about four o'clock, hope dawned with the clattering of china telling me that Harriet, now dressed in her afternoon uniform of black dress and frilly cap and apron, was preparing the tea-trolley. Soon the grown-ups would appear, and we would all sit round the fire and have tea with bread-and-butter, scones, biscuits and cakes.

Sometimes visitors came, usually the same ones, such as my uncles on the way home from work, or close family friends like Sylvia and Phil Gelling. Phil had a tinge of a Birmingham accent and would tease me by exaggerating it and calling me 'Jine', which made me feel uncomfortable. Quite often, and especially when any of my young cousins came to tea, we played cards: Old Maid, Rummy or Lexicon (a sort of pre-Scrabble card game which, good at spelling, I liked best). Auntie Gwen and Granny loved these games, but Grandpa stood at the side, pointing out which card to play but never taking a hand of his own.

A bit later the grown-ups would progress to drinks, mostly gin-and-orange or gin-and-lime (a portion of gin diluted with almost neat orange squash or Rose's Lime Juice)—but sherry on the rare occasions when it was available. And there was always the etched-glass tumbler of whisky and soda on the table beside my grandmother's chair—unusual in the 1940s. She drank it for her health, it was understood.

IT WAS ABOUT this time that a new friend came into my life, my second cousin Valerie Rowed (who later went off caravanning with Karen White). She was two or three years older than me, also an only child, and she had endured an upbringing that in a different way—a highly neurotic mother—was even more difficult than mine. Sometime in the 1990s we met for lunch at the Royal Academy and she recalled that she had loved coming to play with me when we were children because I was even naughtier than she was: I recollect it as being the other way round—certainly, being so much younger, I followed her lead—she would suggest doing something outrageous and I, keen to impress, did it.

One day when she came to Hollywood we climbed up on to the roof of the sewing-room (a single-storey extension from the drawing-room where Auntie Gwen had an old treadle sewing-machine). We hid behind a parapet and threw stones over the holly hedge at vehicles which, from time to time—it was wartime!—passed along the main road in front of us. Quite soon a woman wearing a camel-hair coat belted round the middle spotted us and came into the garden to berate us soundly for such disgraceful behaviour. It simply hadn't occurred to us—or to me anyway—that what we were doing was dangerous and bad, and I was duly ashamed. Auntie Gwen never knew about it of course, as it happened during rest.

It wasn't the end of our stone-throwing, though. In the summer holidays that followed Valerie and I went on an anarchic trip by a series of trams and buses to the Lickey Hills on the other side of Birmingham, and startled courting couples by throwing stones—not at, but near enough to alarm them. But by the next holidays, Valerie was suddenly a teenager and no longer bothered with me.

AT THE SAME time, I was jolted out of my security. At the end of the summer holidays, Auntie Gwen took me up the stairs at the end of the passage to the little old room above the larder. It was untidy but quaint, with an uneven floor and crooked low ceiling and a little window almost at ground level; quite a friendly little room—but by itself, isolated from the rest of the house. Would I like this room to be my very own? she asked. The junk could be cleared out and it would all be made pretty and ready for me when I came home next holidays. I was horrified—it was up its own little staircase—away from the rest of the family. She tried to reassure me: it wasn't really so far from the rest of the house. She opened a cupboard door and pointed to a crack of light at the back of it. 'Look, that's Granny's bathroom you can see through there.' The thought was more alarming than reassuring.

'What about my room?' I asked; my own blue room, where I always slept. The truth of the matter was that it didn't belong to me, it was Auntie Norah's room, and she was coming home and I was to be ousted, not only from the room which I had come to think of as mine (in spite of all those pictures of other children) but even from my place beside Grandpa at table.

IN THE MEANTIME, there was another term. In the seven long years I spent at St Christopher's it is hard to distinguish what happened when, but by this time I was bigger and, even if not quite one of the Big Ones, an established member of the school community—although my hot temper was a barrier to easy relationships. Once, I got in a fight with an older girl. I have no idea how it started but I remember attacking her with gusto and being quite disappointed when we were pulled apart. The older girl got into terrible trouble over it, I discovered many years later.

AROUND ABOUT THEN I wrote a play, *The Tasks of Psyche*, based on the Victorian book of Greek myths and legends we were reading in English. I was the hero, Eros, in a Grecian-style dance tunic, and Jill with her long fair hair was Psyche. Other children were persuaded into playing the dragons and other monsters which Eros had to fight and overcome to win his love. The Big Ones were scornful, but they were made to come and watch it, and the teachers came too. Anybody with any idea of the erotic connotations of these myths would have been doubled up with laughter —but probably even the grown-ups then were innocent of it.

ALTHOUGH PART OF me longed to stay at home and go to day school, I knew that I was getting a much better education than friends like Shirley or my cousin Valerie, who went to a school in Wylde Green where the curriculum was not so remote from Miss Roberts' school for young ladies in Rhyl. St Christopher's was run like a boys' prep school. We started French at six and Latin at eight. We progressed from Sums through Arithmetic to Maths —my chief dislike. There was no laboratory, but there was Nature Study, later dignified as Botany, and I remember growing broad beans on blotting paper inside jam-jars; and a smattering of Physics—we measured the distance of a candle from its counterpart reflected in a piece of glass, and watched metal filings rushing to and then fleeing from the opposite ends of a magnet. There were always lots of books to read, old and new— and I was still starting to write stories just like the one I'd just read. It was a purposeful and interesting education, and we were aiming high: at entrance, perhaps even scholarships, to well-known public schools. When I got to Sherborne School for Girls, I was so far ahead of my contemporaries in most subjects that even though I was put in a class of girls a year or more older than me, my constant complaint was that I had done it all before.

WE STILL SPENT the afternoons outdoors—in winter and spring, hockey or netball on the beach, and in summer, tennis at the club round the corner from the school. We went for walks, nature or otherwise, and at weekends we were let loose on the beach or among the sandhills of what had, before the war, been Burnham and Berrow Golf Links. There we played games like cockyolly or (in the middle of the war against Germany) French and English. More and more of the territory was being lost to the War Department, and they built a huge barbed-wire-fenced enclosure to keep prisoners-of-war in, but somewhat to our disappointment it was never populated.

Once some girls came across a man exposing himself (whatever that meant) among the scrubby bushes of the sand hills, and there was quite a fuss about it. From sheer curiosity, I was disappointed that I was not there. In general, though, I was determinedly childish and innocent. I hated the idea of growing up, even though when I ran my hand over my chest it was no longer completely flat, and I knew what that meant.

SOME SATURDAYS, IF the weather was too bad for us to spend the afternoon in the sand dunes, or for a treat, we went to the Blue Bird Café in the centre of Burnham for exciting baked-beans-on-toast, or to Pope and Churchill, the book-and-stationery shop, or Maynard's sweet shop, to spend our sweet ration.

In the summer every now and then we went further afield, to Cheddar Gorge for example; once we even cycled there to pick strawberries on the steep dusty slopes—it was hard work on a hot day, but you could eat small sweet squashy strawberries as you picked—much more delicious than the solid, made-to-last strawberries we know today. We visited Gough's Cave and the smaller but prettier Cox's Cave with its miniature stalactites and stalagmites lit to look like fairyland.

Nearer to hand was Brent Knoll—a bike ride away and, like Glastonbury Tor, a sudden bump in the level landscape. We used to climb up and run round the rim of its hollow summit. We assumed that it must have been a volcano—no one explained to us that it was an Iron Age camp.

Best of all, in the summer, was the open-air swimming pool

at Weston-Super-Mare, but that meant using part of the petrol ration.

I WROTE TO my parents—and they to me—on airgraphs (*below*), a form of air-letter invented to save space on planes. You wrote on octavo-sized blank forms, which the post office photographed and sent on by air as stamp-sized negatives to their various destinations, where they were enlarged to a final four-by-five inches. I could always read my mother's horizontal scrawl on

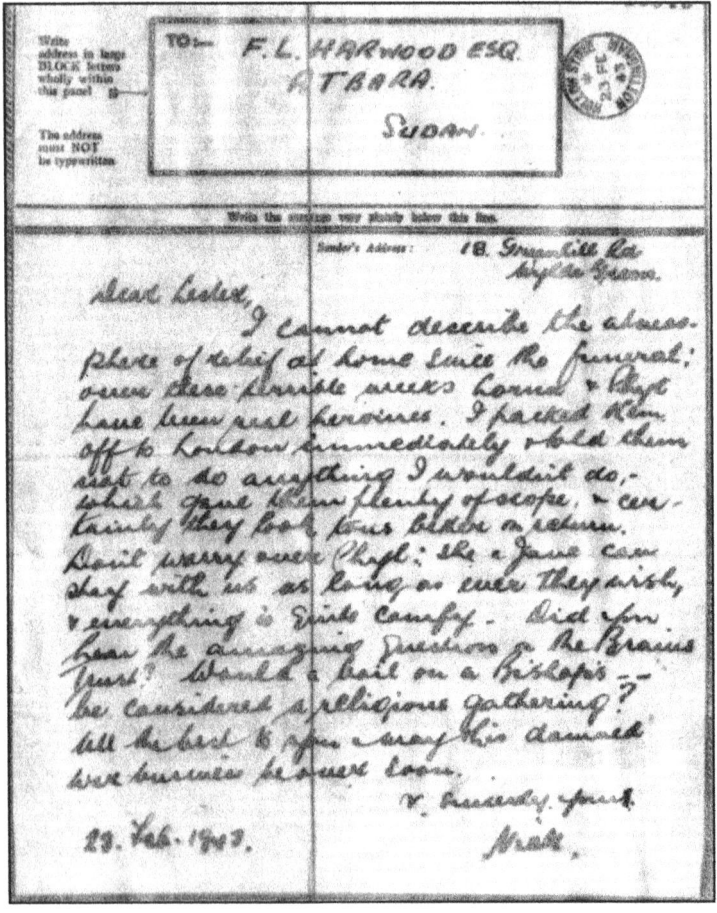

these inadequate scraps of paper but my father's elegant copperplate was much more difficult. He had become very remote to me; I had no memory of what he was like or sense of what he had to do with me.

TIME IS ELASTIC. When school began in late September (as private schools did in those days; something to do with the shooting season I think) the thirteen weeks of the autumn term stretched ahead like a prison sentence, and we were almost as thoroughly incarcerated. The telephone was never used except in an emergency, and parents or relations visited perhaps once a term. Half-term was nothing more than a single day without lessons, or a local outing if the school could manage to organise one. The first weeks of each term dragged on and on without hope—and then, suddenly!—there were only five weeks to go and the sentence began to seem manageable. Everything accelerated towards exams and end-of-term excitements like Christmas, to bring all to a climax. And then it was the last week and time for the great chant of relief:

> This time next week, where shall we be?
> Not in this acadamee!
>
> No more Latin, no more French,
> No more sitting on a hard board bench ...

Pretty traditional and probably going back to Tom Brown's Schooldays: we didn't sit on benches. But local grievances—cockroaches, spiders and cold—added new verses to the St Christopher's version. It wasn't so much that we hated school; it was more the monotony of it and, for me anyway, the effort of keeping my end up for such a very long time.

WHEN I WENT home for the Christmas holidays in 1944 Auntie Norah was at Hollywood and everything was different. I resented—unfairly, I knew—being exiled from 'my' room, which all along I had known was hers, and from my place next to Grandpa at the dining table. I used to glare at her from my exile on the other side of the table (which was far away from the warmth of the gas fire too). I felt she resented my presence as much as I resented hers.

There were lots of odd things about Auntie Norah, including her toes. When she lay in the bath and stretched her long feet up beside the taps, they went: toe, toe, little piece of orange sponge rubber, toe, toe; toe, toe, little piece of orange sponge rubber, toe, toe. As a child I found it odd, but rather fascinating. Looking at it now, why had she, in her twenties or thirties, had a toe removed on each foot? Hammer toes? But her feet didn't twist into the high-instep-hammer-toes shape that mine were assuming. Toes too long? Feet too wide to squeeze, Ugly-Sister-like, into elegant shoes? Perhaps, in the days when many people had all their teeth removed as a matter of course because false ones were so much less trouble, the idea of removing unsatisfactory toes was not so bizarre.

She had illnesses, too—not ordinary illnesses which everyone got, but interesting ones which people talked about, serious illnesses which needed operations, each one followed inevitably by something mysterious called 'lesions'. I don't think it's unfair to say that she used her ill-health to be the focus of attention, and to dominate people. When she had come home in the autumn of 1944, it was for good.

I CAN'T TRUST myself to be entirely fair on Norah Harwood.

She was born in 1906, fourth of five children, nine years younger than Gwen. Like Gwen, she went to Penrhos College and when she left school—notably good-looking, tall, elegant—she agitated to be allowed to do a job. Eventually, my old-fashioned and provincial grandparents relented, and she was allowed to train as a Norland Nurse: Norland Nurses were nice girls trained to look after nice children in nice families, where they were safely chaperoned and would not come to any harm. The social uneasiness of being neither fish nor fowl nor good red herring cannot have occurred to my grandparents; let alone the dangers for a good-looking girl in such a position, which we are more aware of nowadays. She had several jobs, one in Ceylon, another in Kenya, mostly with families connected in some way with her own. She worked in at least one grand family, where the children had to be taught to control their bladders for unnatural lengths of time in preparation for life at court: this was certainly not a family she got to know through friends in the Harwood orbit.

From the start, though, her career was interrupted by bouts of illness, each one more complicated—and interesting—than the last, and in 1944, aged only thirty-eight, she came home to spend the rest of her life as an invalid.

Soon after the end of the war she developed a thyroid condition which Dr Webb, the family's charming GP, failed to recognize and investigate in time. It caused the bones in her head, hands, and feet to swell and made her appearance grotesque. This alone was enough of a tragedy, but there were always other complicated medical problems, and increasingly frequent heart attacks.

There was deep frustration somewhere, a lack of fulfilment. She had intense friendships with women but never, I am sure, any interest in men. Denied a proper emotional outlet, as so often happened in those days, her whole life turned inward and her fascinating illnesses became her occupation, and she used her illnesses to dominate those around her.

Norah's ill-health dictated the course of the rest of Auntie Gwen's life. In 1951, after my grandparents died, Hollywood was sold at auction and being, like The Manor of Pype, a historic and rather beautiful house in the wrong location—Erdington, a Birmingham suburb, rather than in The Royal and Ancient Borough of Sutton Coldfield a quarter of a mile away—nobody wanted it. It went for a pitiful sum and was converted into a care home with all sorts of unattractive annexes added on. It is still there, still called Hollywood. The new owners lost little time in selling the garden and six detached houses were built on it.

The disastrous sale meant that my aunts had much less money than they had expected. They moved to Barton-on-Sea on the south coast, and Auntie Gwen, freed from caring for her parents, had a new burden in looking after her demanding invalid sister who could, my mother reckoned, always produce a heart attack when the occasion demanded.

Norah's life was a drama in which she was the leading player. When people both sisters knew paid a visit, Norah always talked about 'my friends', coming to see 'me'. Incredibly, her greatest satisfaction in her life—as she confided to a diary found after her death in 1973—was having been born a Harwood.

And in spite of having been a Norland Nurse, she was not good with children, my children among them. She demanded love—and there is nothing that children shy away from more.

BY NOW—1944—the war news was positively exciting. I remember pausing at the kitchen door at St Christopher's on D-Day (almost my birthday) and hearing the BBC talking about the Normandy Landings and the amazing floating harbour called Mulberry. After that, we followed the campaigns of the allied armies as they fought their way through France. The wireless was usually on in the kitchen (where Auntie Wattie now did all the cooking) and we clustered round to listen to the six o'clock news on the BBC Home Service every evening, following closely the day-to-day progress—and setbacks—of our armies advancing through France, sometimes with our hearts in our mouths, sometimes exhilarated, as when the troops reached

Paris. The newspapers were full of war news, but there was lots more information—and photographs—in *Picture Post*, including puzzling ones of women with their hair shaved off: 'collaborators'. I found that confusing. From further off, there was news of the Russian army pushing the Germans back round something called the Dnieper Bend.

The war in the Far East was still something to worry about, and at home there was a nasty setback to our confidence when, within days of the D-Day landings, the rockets started, V1s— doodlebugs—and later the much bigger V2s. It was hard to know which was the more frightening: the doodlebugs, which could be heard coming, with the engine liable to cut out at any moment, at which you knew you were done for, or the inaudible V2s which just exploded. But they were a threat I experienced at second hand; I never lived in the areas within their reach.

THAT SUMMER I paid another ill-starred visit to Cheltenham, to stay with the Somervails (the family I should have had lunch with the previous Christmas). They had been friends of my parents in the Sudan and had two daughters, Jane, my age, and Anne, a couple of years older.

The first day I was there I had the shock of my life when I went to the lavatory and found that my knickers were full of blood. I had some vague inkling of what it might be about and decided to cope, which, thanks to the heavy knickers and linings we all wore, and a downstairs lavatory with a washbasin, I did.

At the end of the day I heaved a sigh of relief that I had got through it all and assumed that my life would now return to normal. But the next day the same thing happened, and the next, so I continued to retreat to the lavatory, and rinse and scrub.

On my last day there, we went swimming and I couldn't think of an excuse for insisting on a changing-room of my own; it was getting better at last, anyway, and I thought I could manage. But the older girl caught sight of my knicker-linings; I can remember her shocked face. Nothing was said, but when I got home to Hollywood there had clearly been a telephone call, and a major fuss was on.

'I told you, Gwen,' said Norah triumphantly.

'We all get it,' said Auntie Gwen. 'Auntie Norah gets it, I get it —even Granny used to get it...'

It sounded like a disease.

A few days later I was summoned into the drawing room and found Dr Violet Parks, the Allday family's doctor, and hence mine, sitting in Granny's chair by the fire, plump in a too-tight dun-coloured coat and skirt. She had been summoned to tell me about the facts of life. I can remember my embarrassment, and the feeling that she was embarrassed too, but not a word about the explanation.

I HATED THE whole business. Although I was tall for my age, I had no obvious curves, and looked and was very childish, quite unprepared to face this gross and inconvenient intrusion from the adult world. I wasn't ready to be grown up. I was beginning to like books with a touch of romance in them, but I felt I ought not to. I felt guilty if I went off into a daydream when the boy and girl at the centre of a story drifted off in a boat in the moonlight. I felt it was wrong for me, a child, to read stories with a love interest, by Neville Shute and writers like him. Like most middle-class girls of my age then, I was, and remained for a long time, dangerously ignorant about sex, and male sexuality was something quite beyond my imagination. It was a grown-up world which I was not ready to belong to.

A FEW DAYS after my return from Cheltenham, Auntie Gwen and I set off for Criccieth in North Wales. Going on holiday during the war was not a matter of packing everyone and everything in a car, still less an aeroplane, but a long day of lugging suitcases in and out of crowded trains and changing at a whole series of stations—Shrewsbury, Welshpool, Machynlleth, Dovey Junction—and arriving battered and weary. But it was exciting all the same.

The first thing we saw as we arrived was a convoy of strange-looking vehicles lumbering down the steep main street and then, to our astonishment, plunging straight into the sea and setting off across the bay towards Harlech. They were landing-craft DUKWs (pronounced 'ducks'), presumably practising their landing skills for somewhere on the European coast (although this was several months after D-Day).

The next day, a Sunday, was brilliantly sunny and there were canoes on the little sheltered harbour in the lee of the castle—and I fell in love with Criccieth at once. But it was 31 August, the last day of the summer season, and the next day, as if recognising this, wind and rain lashed sea and hills, and the canoes and deck chairs had all been put away for the winter.

For some reason, the Harwoods took their holidays in September and private schools used to start the autumn term towards the end of that month. In any case, the crowds had gone home by then. Whatever the reason, we used to arrive just in time for the end of the holiday season and the start of the equinoctial gales.

Nevertheless, it was a good holiday. I made a friend, Mavis, who was a Quaker from Selly Oak. In a dismal almost-deserted tea-room by the harbour we played with a slot machine in which the prizes were cigarettes. It was fun winning them but we were not brave enough to try them when we won, so we gave them to the spotty youth who was in charge of the place. More positively, Auntie Gwen and I made excursions to romantic places like Beddgelert and Aberglaslyn. I liked the story of Llewellyn and his faithful dog Gelert (we went and looked at Gelert's grave) and, ever the swot, I was intrigued to find Welsh names with Latin roots like Pont Aberglaslyn and Eglws and Isgol.

One day Auntie Gwen and I walked beyond Beddgelert and I

climbed up between the trees by the road and found myself awesomely alone in bare heather moorland with mountains soaring up in the distance. In the teeth of a warm blustery wind I sang, my voice blending with the wind's: it was a kind of epiphany, a Wordsworthian romantic experience. I was, in spite of my rejection of physical changes, growing up. My sense of what was beautiful was beginning to be different from a child's. I still liked the fairytale prettiness of Cox's Cave at Cheddar and the memory of the coral in Port Sudan, but mountains and moorland were something different—and this identification with nature as a force was thoroughly adolescent.

WE WERE STAYING in lodgings with a Mrs Jones. Auntie Gwen handed over our ration books and discussed with Mrs Jones what we should eat each day, and Mrs Jones did the shopping and cooking. Mrs Jones had been Miss Jones before she had married, and three of her four sisters had married Mr Joneses, the last one spoiling the pattern by marrying a Cadwallader. One of the other Mrs Joneses had a daughter in her mid-teens and we went for a walk together one day, along the railway line to Black Rock. Clearly she had been briefed to Talk to Me, so she did her best, which meant filling me up with all sorts of superstitions about what I should do—and, more importantly not do—during my periods: not putting my feet in water, I seem to remember, and not washing my hair. However, with my naturally sceptical nature I didn't believe a word of it.

After that, no one ever tried to talk to me about sex or growing up, and if I did ask anything there was no answer. I remember being very worried about advertisements in the paper: 'VD is dangerous … . The only solution is absolutely clean living … .' What was this new danger? When I asked the grown-ups, they provided no enlightenment. I lay in the bath and thought about it. What was clean living? Had I washed myself properly? I reached for the soap … .

A year later, when my mother was home again, she left a book about it all, in a place where I would find it and read it, my natural curiosity being the only necessary spur. And needless to say, the subject simply wasn't mentioned at school.

BY THE SPRING of 1945 it was clear that the war in Europe was coming to an end. This was a relief, but to us children it was not a surprise. England (I'm afraid we thought in terms of England) *won* wars—Agincourt, the Armada, the Napoleonic Wars, the Crimean War, the Boer War, the Great War ... . Half the map of the world was the comforting pink of the British Empire, proving that we were the best and greatest nation on Earth.

There is a huge difference between then and now. In the twenty-first century, wherever in the world there is a war or any atrocity, it is pictured immediately in all its living horror. In the 1940s our news came from the wireless, from the occasional fuzzy black-and-white picture in newspapers or better ones in Picture Post, and optimistic newsreels on our occasional visits to the cinema. It is not surprising that we understood so little.

That changed, however, in April 1945 when the British army in Germany captured Belsen, and we saw the first pictures of a concentration camp with the living skeletons of those who had managed to survive the squalor and piles of dead bodies of those who hadn't. It was a shock that no one of my age will forget. Until then, we knew nothing about the death camps or the intended extermination of the Jews of Europe; now we saw for ourselves the monstrous crimes of the Nazis—and we knew that we had been fighting in the cause of right.

And then one day that summer, while I was turning the leaves of a book in Pope and Churchill's book shop in Burnham, the thought suddenly struck me for the very first time: our victory hadn't been inevitable; we might have been defeated ... . We might have had the Gestapo, persecution of the Jews, the death camps ... . Belsen might have been in Britain ... . We might have become part of the Nazi empire ... . The dark possibility shook me to the core.

VICTORY IN EUROPE—VE Day, 8 May, 1945—came on the very day of the Sherborne scholarship exam. They gave me a chair and table in a bedroom at the top of the house, and I had to get on with it. I could hear the distracting noise of distant shouting and laughter and, a strange new sound, church bells: for six long years church bells had been silenced, only to be used as a warning of invasion. In the evening, exams done, I went with all the other boarders to a bonfire party in a day girl's house.

Auntie Wattie used to read to us Big Ones in her drawing room every evening before we went to bed. Immediately after VE Day, she started us on a new book—*Emil and the Detectives*. We looked at each other in astonishment: this was about the adventures of a German boy. I think her choice illustrates how special the Watson sisters were.

A WEEK OR two later Auntie Wattie drove me to Sherborne to be interviewed for the open scholarship. All the candidates had sessions with various teachers in the big oak-panelled hall and then went one by one to see the Headmistress, the alarming Miss Hilda Violet Stuart. She was quite nice to me.

'What do you want to be when you leave school?' she asked.

'An architect,' I said. I liked the idea very much and I knew that my father approved (I must have got something out of those elegantly illegible airgraphs).

She looked at my marks on the sheet in front of her.

'No,' she said. 'You can't do that. Your arithmetic isn't good enough.' Thus are our destinies prescribed for us. I have always half-regretted it.

We all had lunch in the boarding-houses for which we were destined. It was a polite and painful meal.

'How do you think you've done?' someone asked me. I said I

thought I had won the scholarship—Miss Stuart had told me I had—but the other girls thought I was just being cocky and it did me no good when I arrived at the school the next term.

After the interviews, standing by the noticeboards in the school entrance hall, Auntie Wattie told me that my mother and father had arrived in England the day before and I was to spend a week with them at home. I jumped for joy—then checked myself halfway through my jump with the thought, 'I'm too big to jump for joy now'. But I was pleased.

By the time we got back to Burnham, a telegram had arrived confirming that the scholarship was mine. All in all, it was a day to remember.

10. My Father

THE NEXT MORNING, I met my father at Templemeads Station in Bristol. I wasn't at all sure what he looked like and scrutinised all the men coming along the platform towards me, but when I saw him, tall and big-built, with white hair and a sunburnt face, there was no mistaking him. We got into the train for Birmingham and tried politely to think of something to say to each other. He was a total stranger to me, and I even more to him—the six-year-old child he had left behind had turned into an awkward young woman. We had nothing in common. We were still strangers when we arrived at Snow Hill, and for a long time afterwards.

He was a clever, complex man, but reserved, certainly with me—and neither of us made much of the other during my week of unexpected holiday. But I had a quick glimpse of another side to him—his uproarious love of comedy. One day during that week we went to see a Laurel and Hardy film—I think they were in the French Foreign Legion—and he laughed so much, swaying backwards and forwards, that I was afraid that he was going to break the whole row of seats. I clung on to my seat and tried with all my twelve-year-old strength to anchor the row to the floor.

A few years later, when we were living in Gerrards Cross, he saw that Max Miller, the Cheeky Chappie, legendary master of the filthy innuendo, was performing in Slough ... so off we went.

My father in Derudeb, Sudan. December 1923.

Lester Harwood, born 31 December, 1899, was the eldest of three sons and a literary man manqué. He shone at school, the King Edward VI in Birmingham, both scholastically and on the rugby field, but at home he was something of a rebel. He wanted to study literature and the classics, but my grandfather would have none of it: 'the Modern Side'—mathematics and science—was what his sons had to do and fathers were all-powerful in those days.

He longed to go to university, but this was also regarded as a waste of time and money: a good business career in one of the family firms was what he was destined for.

However, he escaped. After a brief spell as an officer cadet in the wartime Navy, he went off to London and got himself articled to a major firm of civil engineers, McAlpine's, leaving his brothers to take his place, one at World's Wear, the other at SC Larkins.

Soon after he qualified, he put even more distance between him and his family. One day on the Underground he met a friend who told him that the Colonial Office was recruiting civil engineers to work in the (then Anglo-Egyptian) Sudan. He went there straight away, was interviewed, got a job, and was soon ordering his tin trunk and tropical gear ready for life in the desert.

The British, who in practice ran the officially designated Anglo-Egyptian Sudan for the first half of the twentieth century, had established the headquarters of Sudan Railways at Atbara, where the River Atbara runs into the Nile, and the line to Port Sudan on the Red Sea branches off the main line to Cairo. He spent most of his time in Atbara but was based at other remote out-stations in the early part of his career.

Life in the desert was not always romantic or exciting, if his poem from the time is anything to go by:

SUDAN AFTERNOON

The still afternoon wears on;
There is no sound but the buzzing of the flies
And the lazy murmur of the labourers
    squatting in the shade.

Every way stretches the flat, gravelly land
With little acacia bushes dotted here and there.
Soon the wind will rise, a steady, tired wind,
    a bored moan.

Nothing will happen.
A few blades of grass will grow and wither,
A little dust will be blown along.
The trees will put forth a little green—
    but not for long.

Nature is bored here.
    God is bored with this land.

But there were upsides too. There were opportunities and far more responsibility than a young man of his age would have got at home. He enjoyed the camaraderie of colonial life in Atbara. He learned Arabic. He made friends with Sudanese colleagues—mostly then junior or even apprentice engineers—to a much greater extent than most of his British colleagues did. He enjoyed the lonely freedom of travelling round the vast railway network in a 'saloon', a sort of railway caravan, to inspect the lines, spot signs of trouble and organise repairs; in a country where everything is built on sand, violent desert rainstorms and suddenly rising rivers regularly wash rails, sleepers and embankments away. My mother loved going with him on these trips.

My parents were married in 1927 and my mother's first home as a married woman was, according to my father's diary, 'a C-type quarter in the middle of Khartoum station', living on 45 Egyptian pounds a month. (By 1931 his pay had risen to £E60 a month but then it was hit by the 7.5% reduction imposed on the whole Civil Service as a result of the slump. When they left the Sudan at the end of 1947, he had 'only a few hundred pounds in the bank'. The thought of penury always haunted him.)

TOWARDS THE END of 1927, to save money (or simply to get out of Khartoum station) my father accepted a posting as District Engineer in Gedaref, capital of the province of the same name bordering Eritrea and Abyssinia. There were few opportunities to spend money in Gedaref—indeed life there was sufficiently tough to carry a hardship allowance. The hardships included 'sharing a one-roomed wooden hut with a swarm of bees ... and hyenas howling round all night', as well as amoebic dysentery, malaria—and hay fever from the elephant grass which grew in abundance and brought on sneezes to match, still without antihistamines to ease them. Quinine used in large quantities to cure my mother's malaria was a cause of her severe deafness in later life.

The Sudan Defence Force's Eastern Arab Corps was based in Gedaref and the Officers' Mess was a pleasant refuge from the wooden hut (they soon moved to more acceptable quarters). The officers, says my father in his diary, were 'an extraordinarily nice lot and very lavish with food and drink. A bagpiper usually played during dinner ... .'

One day the SDF commander, a Major Walsh, asked my father to have a look at their well, which was running dry. The diary records what happened:

> The well was about four foot in diameter. I hung a home-made rope ladder down and climbed to near the bottom. The cause was clear:

the suction pipe did not reach the water. I then tried to climb up again but found I was sweating and could not climb the ladder, which was swinging about in a very awkward way.

He could have died from the fumes at the bottom of the well but a young officer in the SDF climbed down and rescued him: this was Orde Wingate, later the legendary leader of the Chindits in Burma. 'A strange personality, absolutely fearless, very unconventional and direct in his way of speech,' my father recorded.

It is a fact that I and all my descendants could well owe our existence to this heroic but maverick and controversial figure who pulled my father out of the well that day.

PROBABLY IN THE early 1930s my father wrote a play, a Cowardesque comedy of marital infidelity and reconciliation through guile. It involves a young engineer coming home on leave from Africa and finding that his wife—who has returned

My mother in Sudan, with an admirer.

ahead of him—is dallying with a former flame. The hero uses a confidante of his own—a sort of older wiser *femme fatale*—to win her back again. It is witty and coherent, very much a period piece. He gave it to me to read when I was at Oxford and I found it puzzling; the light-hearted and distinctly amoral young man in the play was so far from the sober churchgoing father I knew ... and yet it was clear that the two were the same.

At the end of my father's play, the young husband wonders why his wife is straying. Something is missing for her in the marriage, he decides, and the only way to keep her contented is to overcome his own reluctance to procreate and let her have a baby. Hence, I reckon, in 1933, after six years of marriage: me.

DURING THE WAR, Orde Wingate, back in the Sudan after years in Palestine, very possibly played a part in my father's story again.

His very well-connected family were converts to the Plymouth Brethren and Orde was an Old Testament Zionist throughout his life, an outsider in any normal environment, an isolated day-boy at Charterhouse and, perhaps above all, in the officers' mess. But he was an original thinker with almost mesmeric powers of persuasion and it was helpful that his uncle, Sir Reginald Wingate, was a legend in the area, having succeeded Kitchener as Governor General of the Sudan and later as High Commissioner in Egypt. With this access, Orde managed to convince the great and good—Wavell, even Churchill himself—of the merits of his own very imaginative and unorthodox strategies for winning the war. His Abyssinian campaign was the first of these.

Abyssinia, now Ethiopia, had been an Italian colony since the middle 1930s. When in 1940 Mussolini declared war on Hitler's side, there was suddenly the danger that the Italian army based there would launch an attack on the Sudan, which was poorly defended, and throw its weight into the Axis Desert War campaign from the south, as it was already doing from another

Italian colony, Libya, in the west. It was clearly an emergency. The SDF recruited and trained local militias—my father was a corporal in the Atbara force—but their numbers were few and their weaponry was inadequate to say the least: the only aeroplane that ever flew low enough over Atbara for its militia to take pot shots at turned out to be British.

In Cairo and Khartoum, the military top brass got to work on planning a campaign to oust the Italians and restore the exiled Emperor Haile Selassie to his throne, and essential to these plans was a railway across 100 miles or so of wild and hilly terrain between Gedaref and the Abyssinian border.

My father was given the job of building this important supply line. He appointed a Sudanese engineer, Mohammed Fadl, as his chief assistant and they immediately started assembling the necessary materials and recruiting wherever they could to find labour. Early in 1941, in utmost secrecy, they began the prodigious task of surveying a route, levelling the ground, clearing the bush, building culverts, embankments and bridges, and then laying the railway, at the rate of more than a mile a day. But the line was never used: the military campaign it was to have been part of was abandoned.

My father, in the bush.

THIS MAY WELL have been because Wingate got there first. With the support of Churchill's SOE in London and Wavell in Cairo (and bypassing altogether the local military command) he put together a 'Gideon Force' of 1700 men: adventurers like Wilfrid Thesiger and Laurens van der Post, irregulars, friends, heroes all —and flew them over the mountains into Abyssinia. Within a few months, this improvised army had roused the local tribes and defeated an Italian army of 15,000, and Wingate was riding into Addis Ababa at the head of a peaceful procession to restore the Emperor Haile Selassie to his country and to his throne. Only then did the Military Headquarters in Khartoum and Cairo learn of the expedition.

They were furious. On his return to base Wingate was greeted with cold resentment. The only official letter awaiting him was to inform him that his temporary promotion to the rank of Lt-Colonel had come to an end and he was now Major Wingate again.

Before long, however, a General at last, he was off on his final and most famous exploit, the daring but controversial Chindit campaign in Burma, which landed irregulars far behind the Japanese lines to attack them from the rear. It had its successes, particularly in damaging Japanese morale, but many questioned its overall contribution to the war. In March 1944, Wingate was killed when a plane carrying him back from his Chindit territory crashed in Manipur. It is said that in the messes of the 14th Army glasses were raised in silent relief.

MY FATHER HAD a good career in the Sudan and was justifiably disappointed when his application to become General Manager of the Railways was unsuccessful. He was 'only' an engineer and such top-level jobs went to members of the elite Political Service.

He was well respected socially too—by his Sudanese friends and the European community alike. He could be very good company and had a much-appreciated talent for churning out amusing and witty commentary on events or people, in clever Hilaire Belloc-type verse, with intricate rhyme-schemes and ironic punchlines.

SUDAN DANCES

After the ballot Cairo dances:
Dancing softened the Sudanese.
Dinka and Nuba the dance entrances,
Whirling canvassers win with ease—
Skipping and hopping the Shilluk please
(Not knowing what voting is all about)
And Salem, the dancing major, prances—
Egypt has danced Great Britain out!

Britain sportingly took her chances,
Keeping from party conflict clear,
Counting on Sudanese 'advances',
Left the voters their course to steer.
Khartoum declined to electioneer
By propaganda or secret bribes—
Britain's conduct her fame enhances—
But dancing captured the southern tribes.

Seldom the British diplomat dances,
Never dances without a coat;
The Foreign Office official glances,
Glances askance at the dancing vote—
Could he pirouette among tribes remote?
His chief and colleagues would think him mad!
But under prevailing circumstances
Things might be better if he had … .

These verses, with their dancing rhythm, lament British officialdom's inability to unbend, which lost them vital elections after the war when the Egyptians used a 'dancing diplomat' to win the Dinka and Nuba tribes of today's South Sudan to their side.

WHEN HE RETIRED from Sudan Railways, my father, aged forty-eight and a Fellow of the Institute of Civil Engineers, embarked on a new career in London with a firm of consulting engineers, Lewis and Duvivier, whose speciality was sea defences. He soon became a partner but his old worries about money came back to haunt him—in particular, liability for a share of the firm's debt—and so in 1960 he resigned his partnership and became a consultant, and he and my mother moved from London to an inconvenient bungalow in an idyllic, solitary position in Devon with huge views across a wide valley to distant Dartmoor.

This was one of the happiest periods of my parents' lives. The local gentry made them welcome, greeting them with visiting cards in pre-war style. There were sherry parties, bridge, golf, the WI, the church, amazing walks and, during the Easter and summer holidays, grandchildren. Lewis and Duvivier provided my father with enough work to keep him as busy as he wanted to be—among other things he travelled round the country to inspect sea defence works and RNLI boat houses and slipways; but he had plenty of time for the absorbing pastime of his later life—fly-fishing in the rivers and pools of Dartmoor. And they never tired of the view.

There was a bonus. Over the years many former colleagues, British and Sudanese, came to visit them, foremost among them Sayed Mohammed Fadl who, nearly twenty years after my father's retirement and now General Manager of Sudan Railways, invited him and my mother to the opening of a new line to the far south-west of the country. They were given VIP treatment and flown round in the President's plane. It was a wonderful and touching tribute. Sayed Mohammed Fadl often came to stay with my parents, right up to the end of my father's life.

Sadly, the Devon idyll did not last long. After only six years or so, Parkinson's disease took over my father's life—before there was even dopamine to relieve its symptoms. My parents moved to the much more ordinary but accessible New Forest, where my mother looked after him devotedly until the end. He was seventy-five when he died. My mother wrote a poem about her love for him.

> I loved him with lilac, dark, pale and white
> And with Easter lilies and crocus
> I loved him with songs well remembered
> And with tales re-told.
> I loved him with evenings of sunsets and serenity
> And with red roses.

NOT LONG AFTERWARDS my mother, who could not cope with living alone, went to live with Auntie Gwen in Barton-on-Sea: my two mothers, the two most important people in my childhood. It worked well to begin with, but they were an ill-suited couple. Auntie Gwen was gentle, quiet, and methodical—but she had claws. Her world was narrow, but she was confident in it. In contrast, my mother, in spite of her much wider experience, her happy marriage, her energy and enterprise, even gallantry, was curiously insecure and could be touchy and outspoken; but she was never mean. She had a loving heart, but the Sarsons vinegar was always present. I was used to it and I could cope with it, but my children found it hard to bear. As the two women grew older—both lived into their nineties—the lubrication of everyday politeness grew thinner and they tended to bicker. But they stuck together until almost the end of their lives.

11. End of an Era

AFTER THAT SPECIAL week with my new-found parents in 1945, I went back to school. It was an exciting end to the term. The war was over—or at least the war in Europe, which was closest to us—and other people's fathers as well as mine were coming back home from prisoner-of-war camps and active service abroad. Several of us had won scholarships to our senior schools, and we celebrated with an outing to the swimming baths at Weston. It was the end of my seven long years at St Christopher's—I should be sad, I said to myself, wandering through the rose garden, I should be crying—but I wasn't. It was time to move on.

BACK HOME IN the Midlands for the holidays, I found all my relations in a state of horror and despair. The general election had taken place, and Attlee and his bunch of dangerous socialists had ousted Winston Churchill, the great hero of the war. In my grandfather's eyes it was treachery, pure and simple. The working classes and the reds, the illiterate Ernest Bevin and the Welsh demagogue Aneurin Bevan, backed up by class traitors like Clement Attlee and Sir Stafford Cripps, had conspired to overturn the Conservatives and deny Mr Churchill the fruits of victory. Not surprisingly, at just twelve, I went along with these views and joined in the general gloom. It all seemed very unfair.

And we were still at war. Now that I had at last realised that it wasn't inevitable that we should win, I started to worry about what was happening in the Far East. There didn't seem to be any good reason for the war there ever to end, and soldiers returning from Germany and even from prisoner-of-war camps faced the prospect of having to go to the jungles of the east to fight against the Japanese—terrifying semi-human fanatics according to the popular press. Stories were getting back about the Burma Road and the infamous prisons of Singapore. At least, people said, the Germans knew the rules of war and they treated their prisoners properly (Belsen and Auschwitz didn't seem to count).

AND THEN, SUDDENLY, it was all over. An atom bomb was dropped, and then another, and we had peace. At the time it seemed like a miracle, an unexpected deliverance from a war that could have dragged on for years, but even at the beginning there was unease.

'It's a new kind of bomb, darling, for the benefit of mankind.'

We saw horrifying pictures of the devastation in Hiroshima and Nagasaki. We celebrated, but somehow the celebrations were muted. Auntie Lorna flew her Union Jack on the flagpole outside the house but it looked a bit odd. There was a huge party outside Sutton Coldfield Town Hall and we danced, but where were the scenes of wild excitement?

Siegfried Sassoon's poem *Everyone Sang* encapsulated my mother's memory of the ending of the First World War:

> Everyone suddenly burst out singing;
> And I was filled with such delight
> As prisoned birds must find in freedom
> Winging wildly across the white
> Orchards and dark green fields;
>   on—on—and out of sight.
>
> Everyone's voice was suddenly lifted,
> And beauty came like the setting sun.
> My heart was shaken with tears; and horror
> Drifted away ... O, but everyone was a bird;
> And the song was wordless;
>   the singing will never be done.

VJ Day was not like that, especially for old-fashioned middle-class families like mine. There was huge relief, but daily life was every bit as hard as it been during the war and there was an added sense of foreboding about the social revolution which now seemed inevitable. Everybody looked back—for many years—to a golden age called 'before the war'.

As for me, it was the end of an era. My parents were going away to the Sudan again and I was facing the frightening prospect of a huge new school and a well-founded fear of not fitting in. It took me a long time before I found the positive and cheerful person that I became.

I too wrote a poem, which was printed in the school

magazine. It is stylised and derivative, and the feeling is the product of films and books rather than experience—but no less felt for that.

> Gone, and whither we know not.
> When last you were here you were young,
> But you flew away at the end of the day
> And the song of your life was sung.
>
> Gone and whither you knew not.
> You knew not that you then must go—
> You did not take, for the last time's sake,
> Looks at loved things here below.
>
> Gone and whither we know not
> We knew not what we would lack
> When you flew away at the end of the day—
> You were gone, and you never came back.